T0484526

Selected Fine Art Photographs

Decades of being around accomplished talent producing absolutely phenomenal quality work has taught that we are capable of greatness. It is possible to meet our destiny and become it. Experiencing excellence done with such apparent ease and humble selfless gratification is the motivation for this photography. Most important was having the freedom

Being colorblind gives an advantage when composing black & white… less confusion. This special collection selected from thousands of captures. All images were framed in the camera and presented without edits, genuine as seen through the lens. RAW conversion applied by proprietary panchromatic process.

Limited edition prints available from original source files.

info@ BEACHNOISE.com

Joseph Fleming

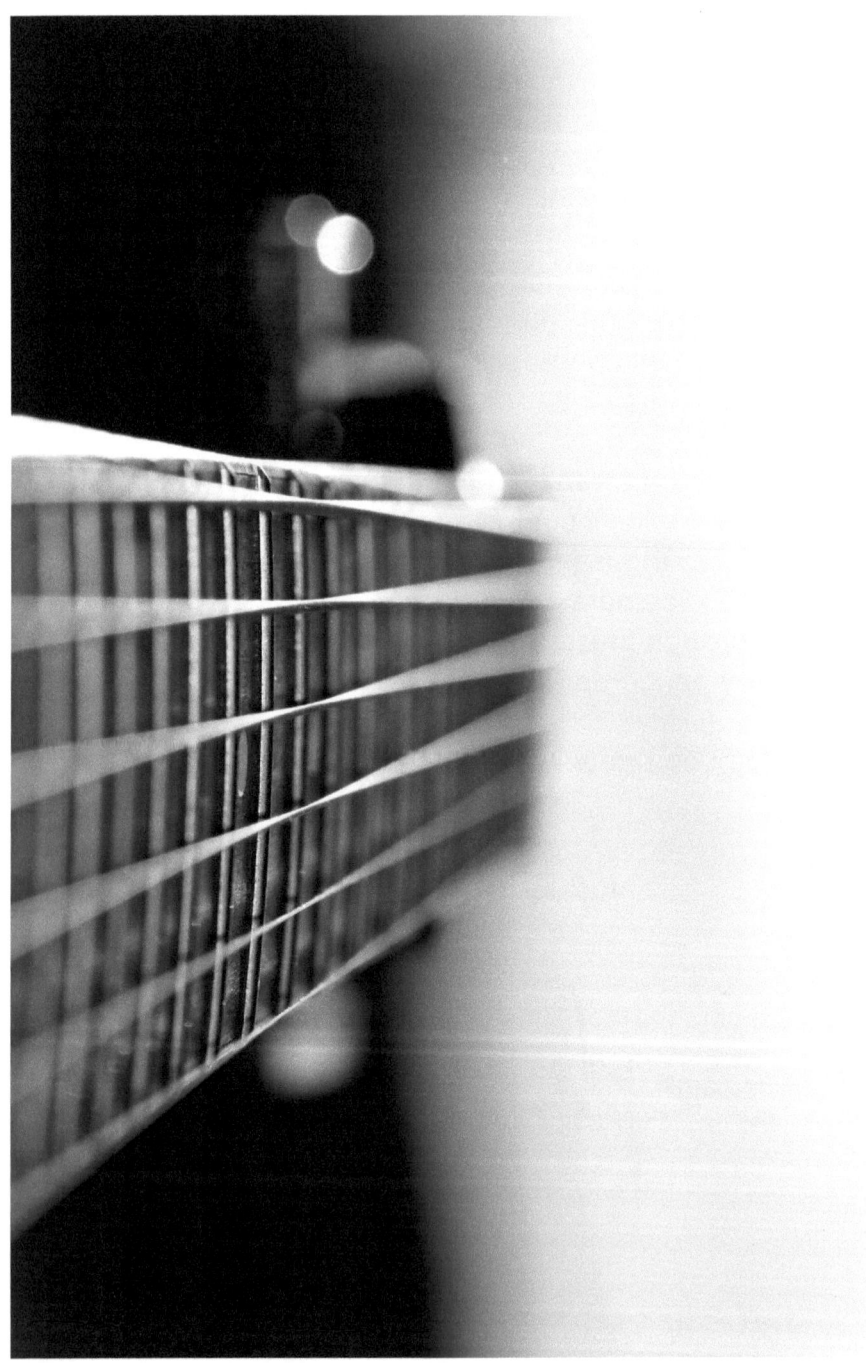

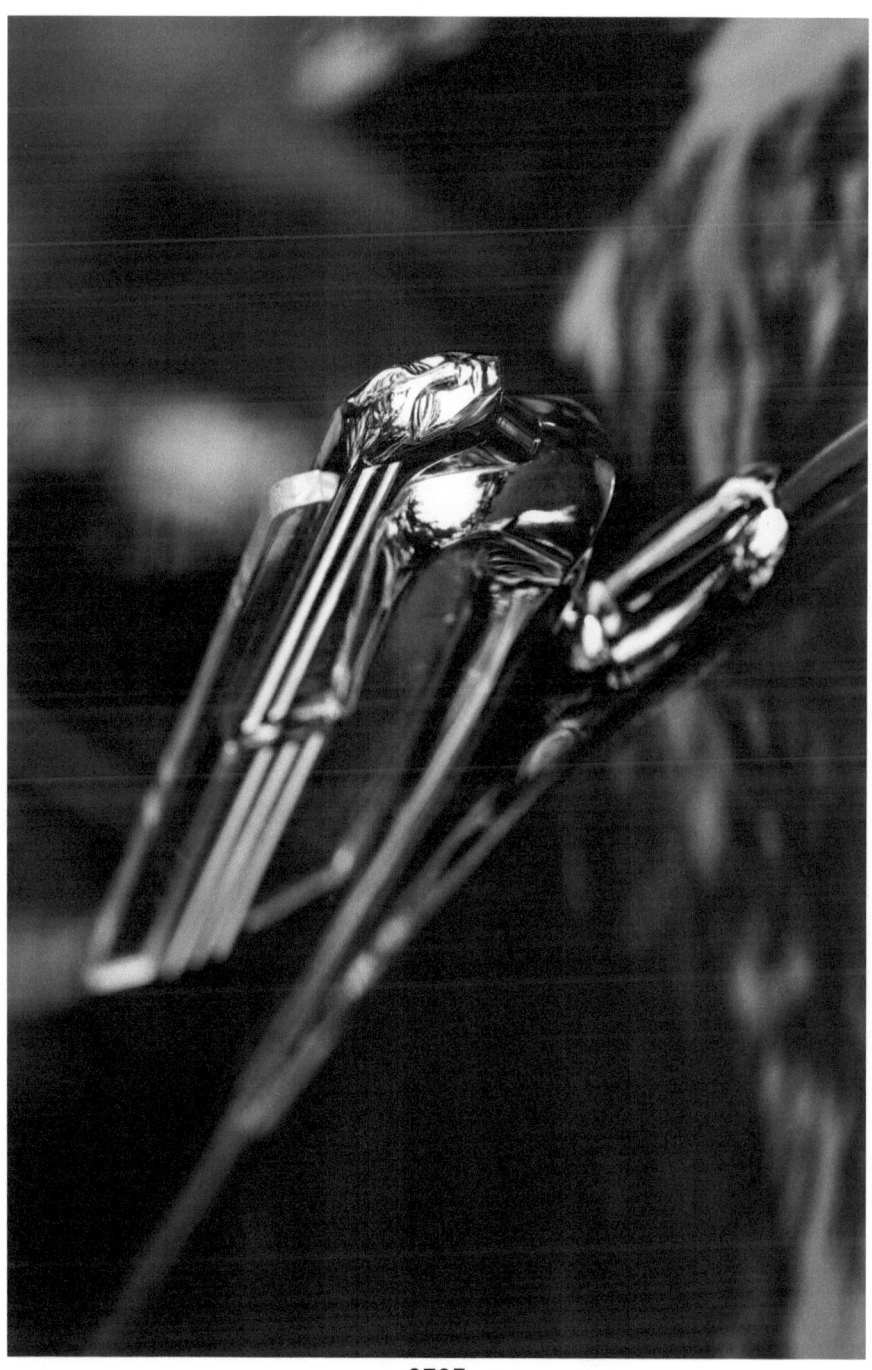

0705

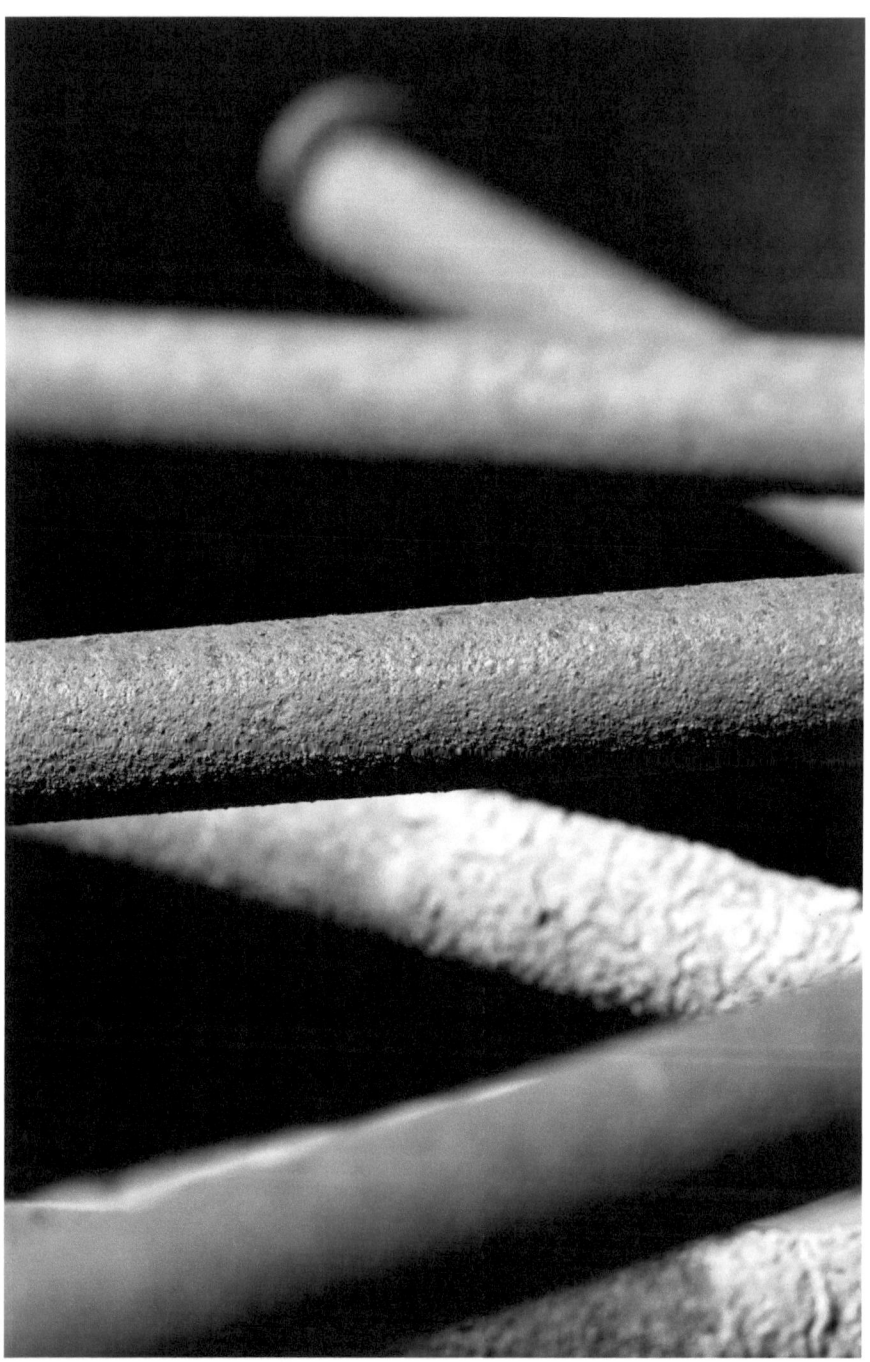

0780

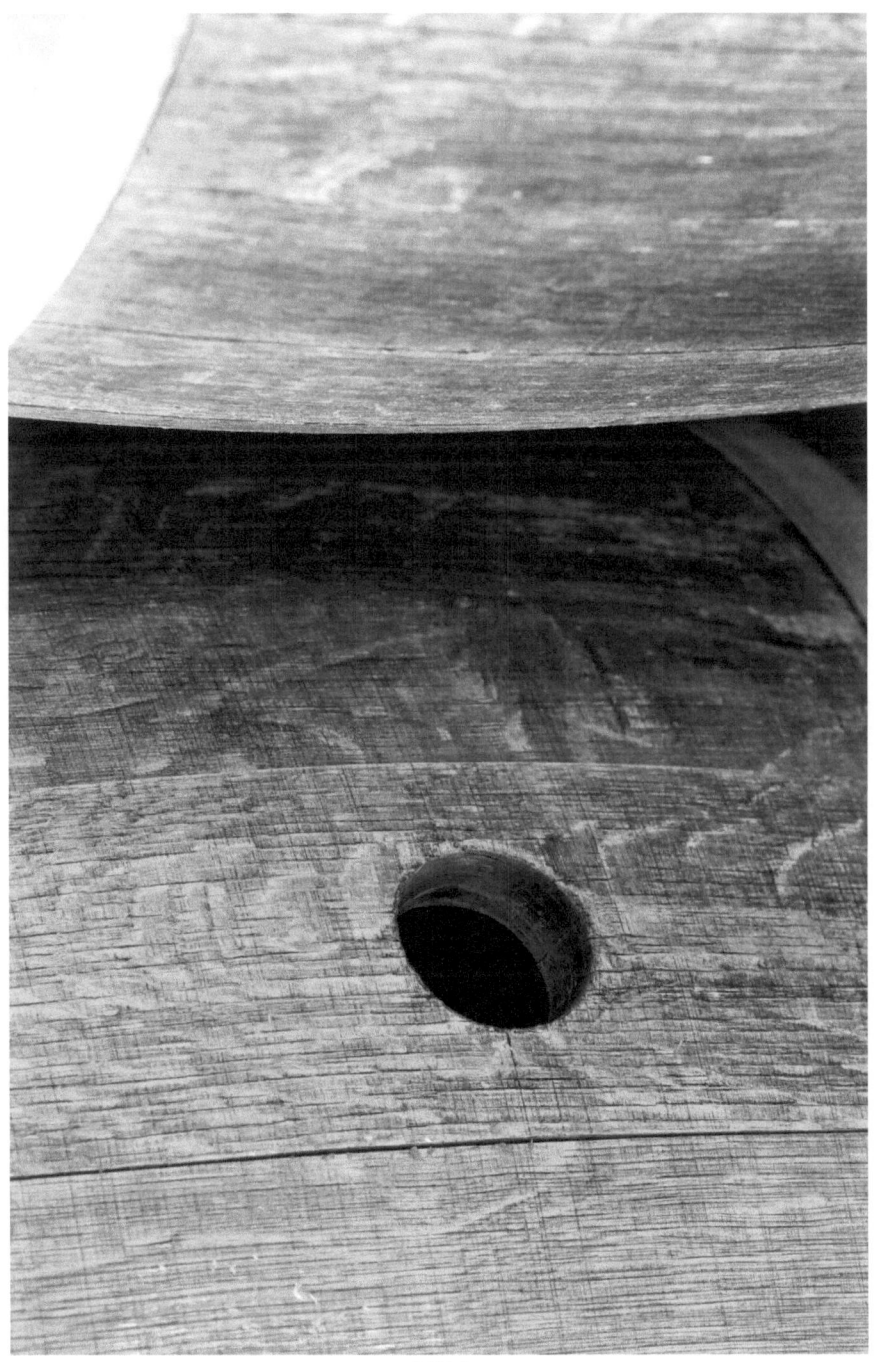

0826

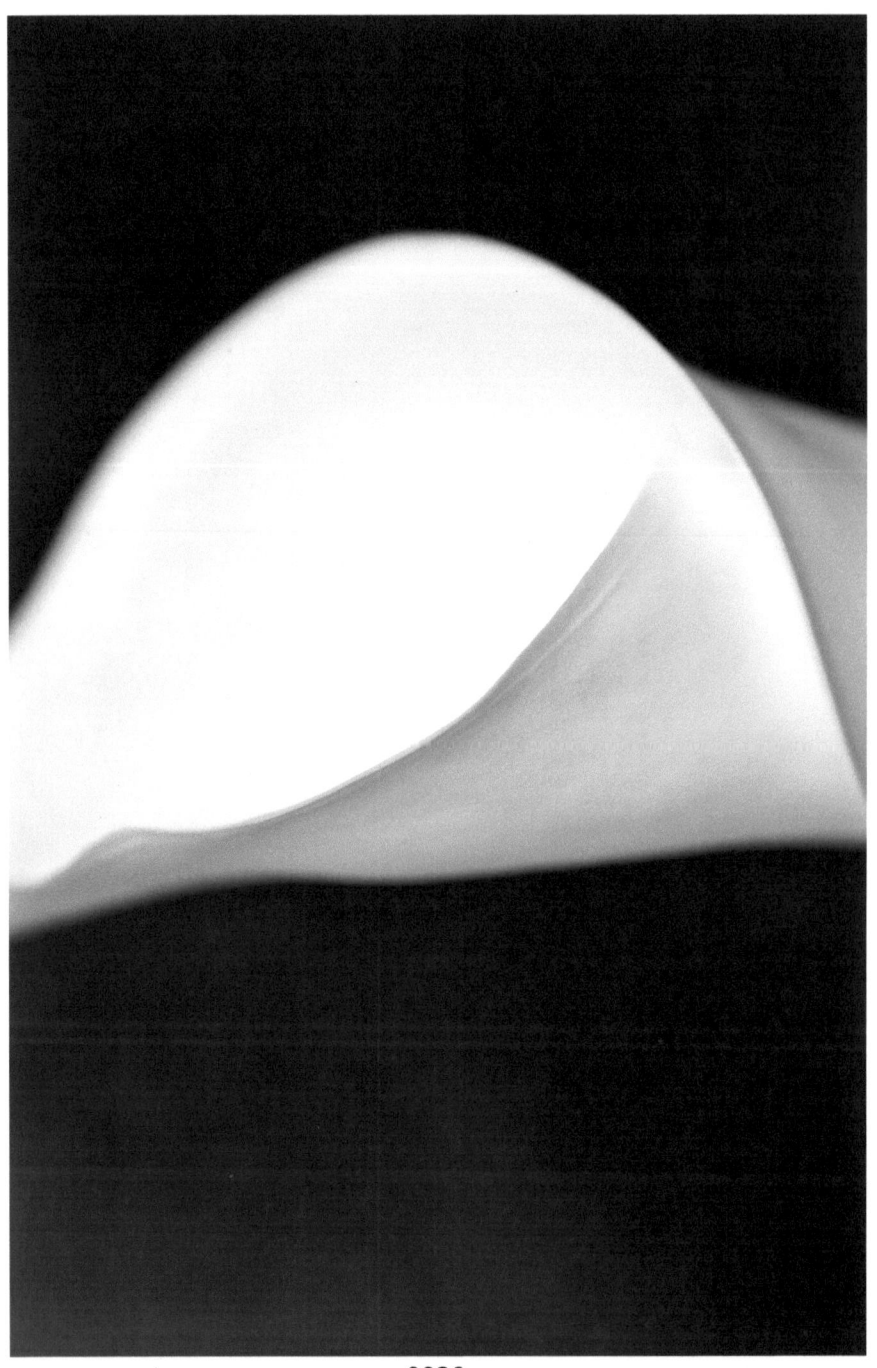

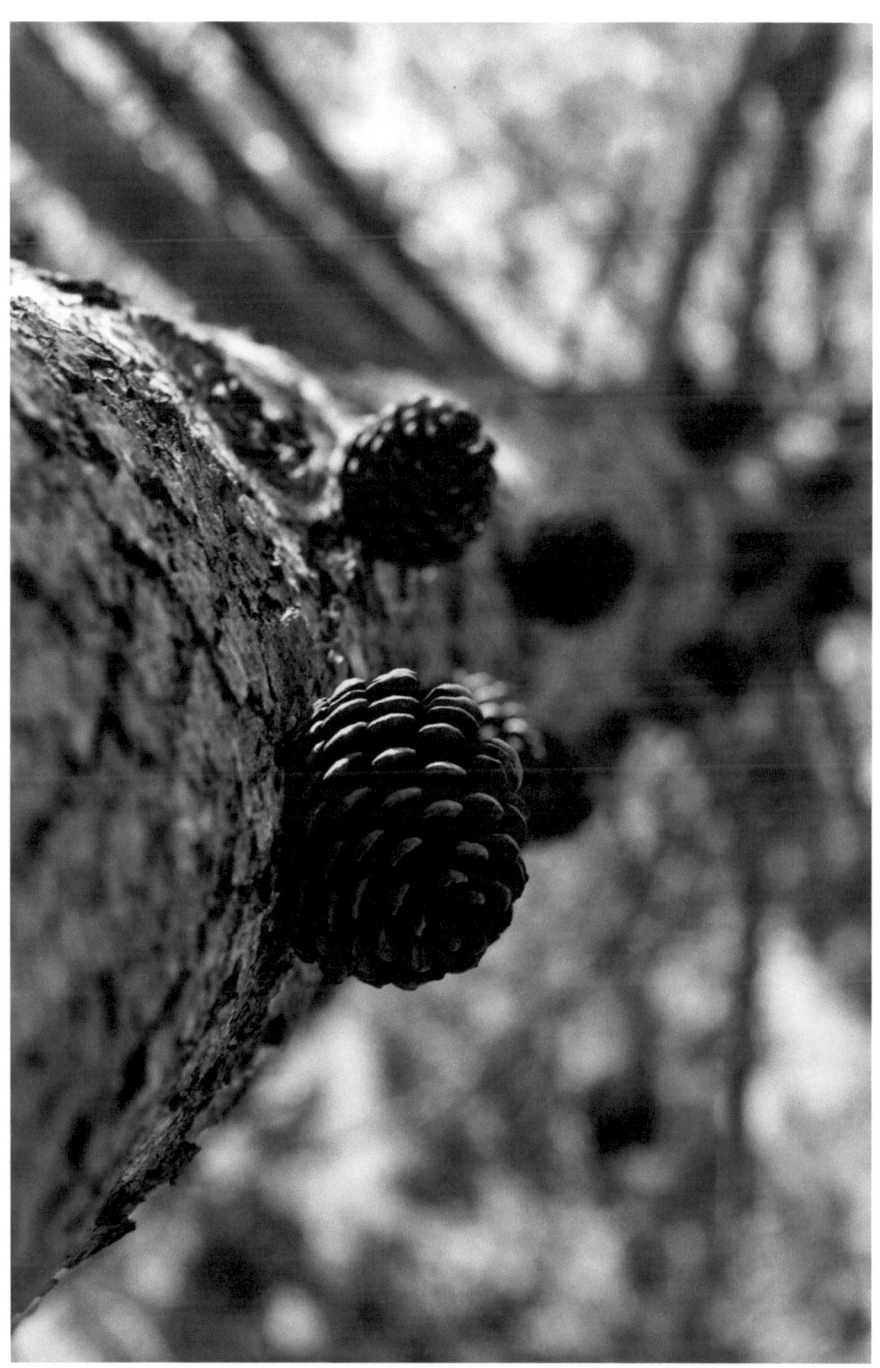

0938

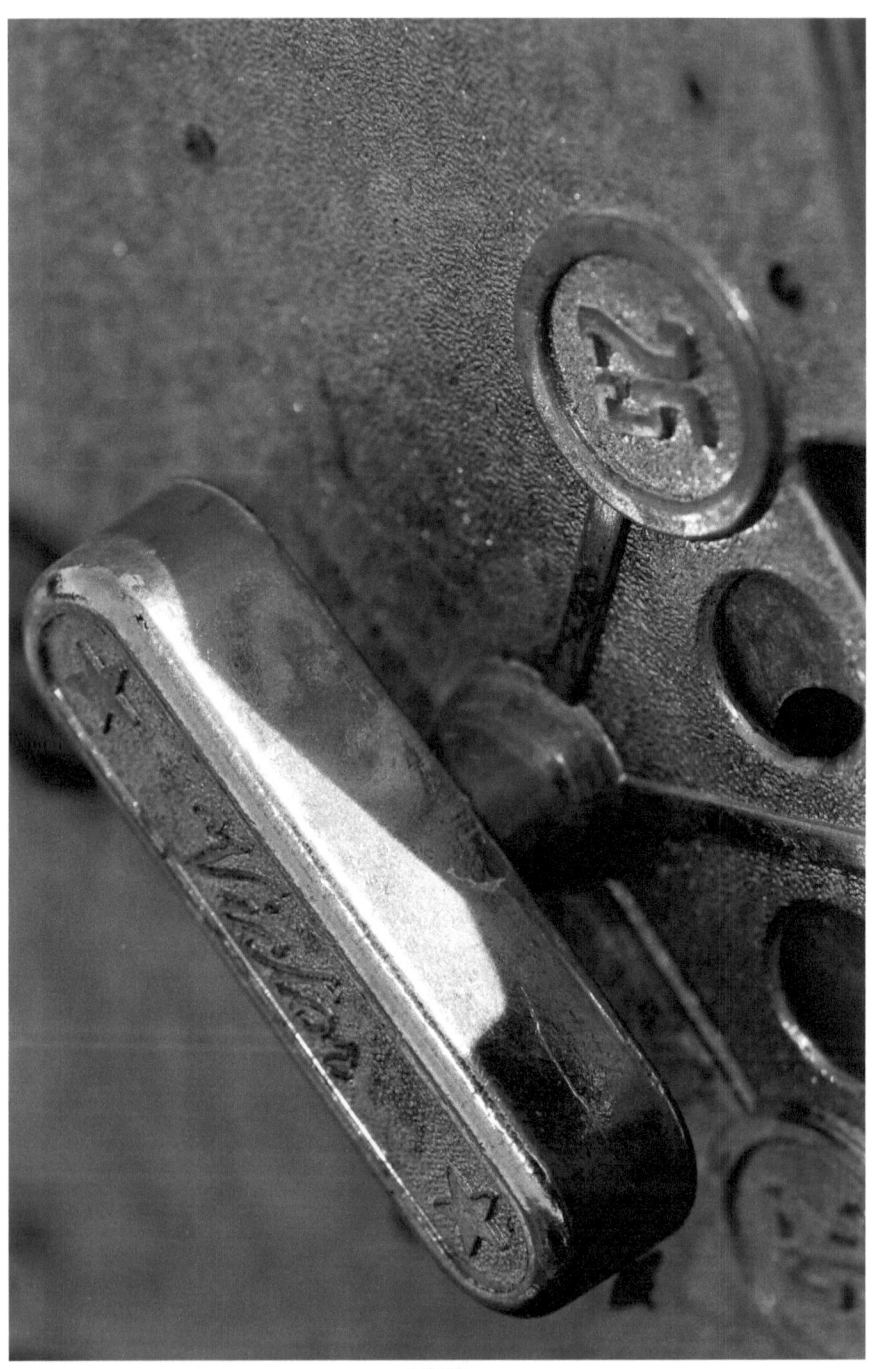

1085

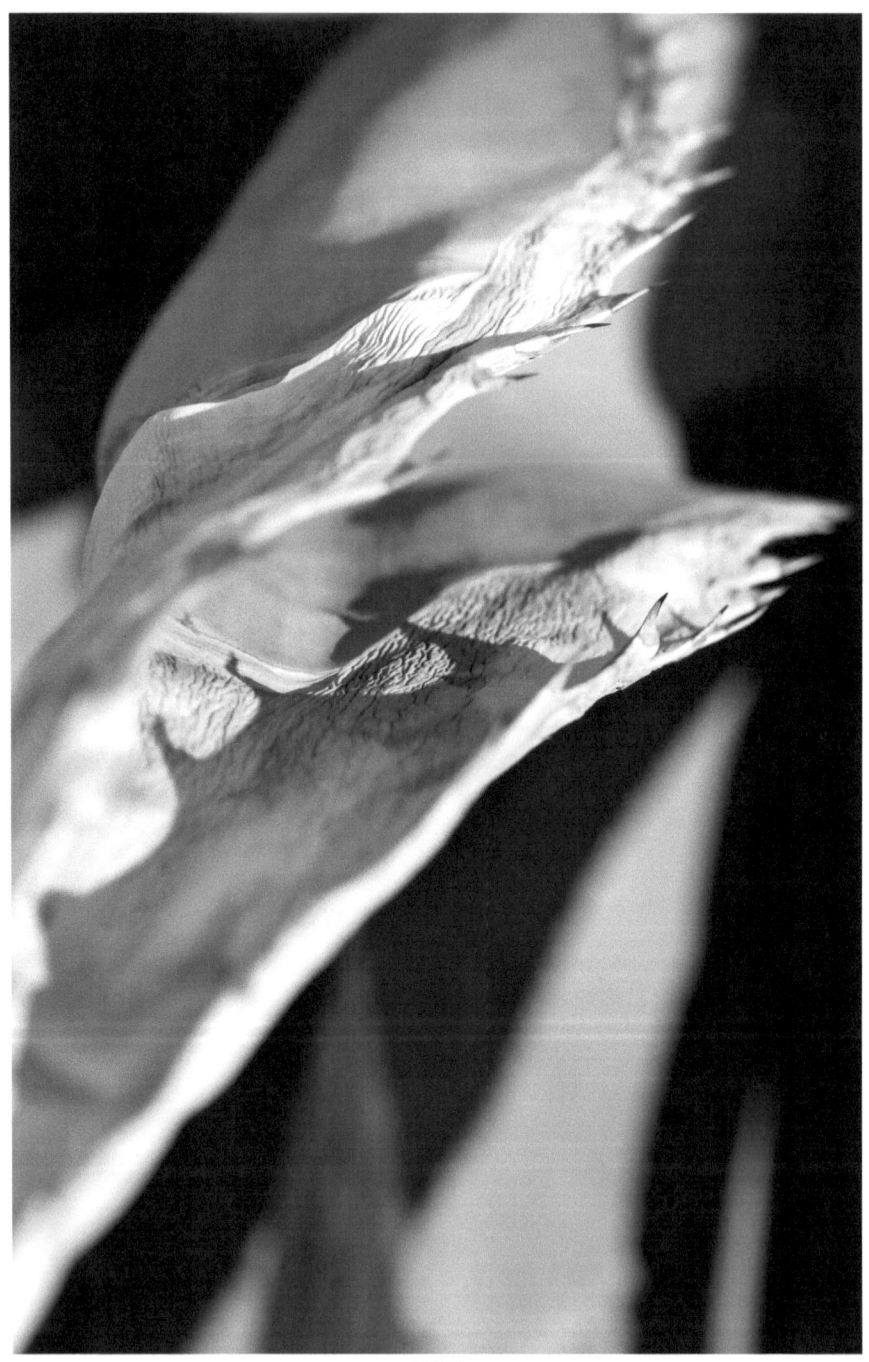

1581

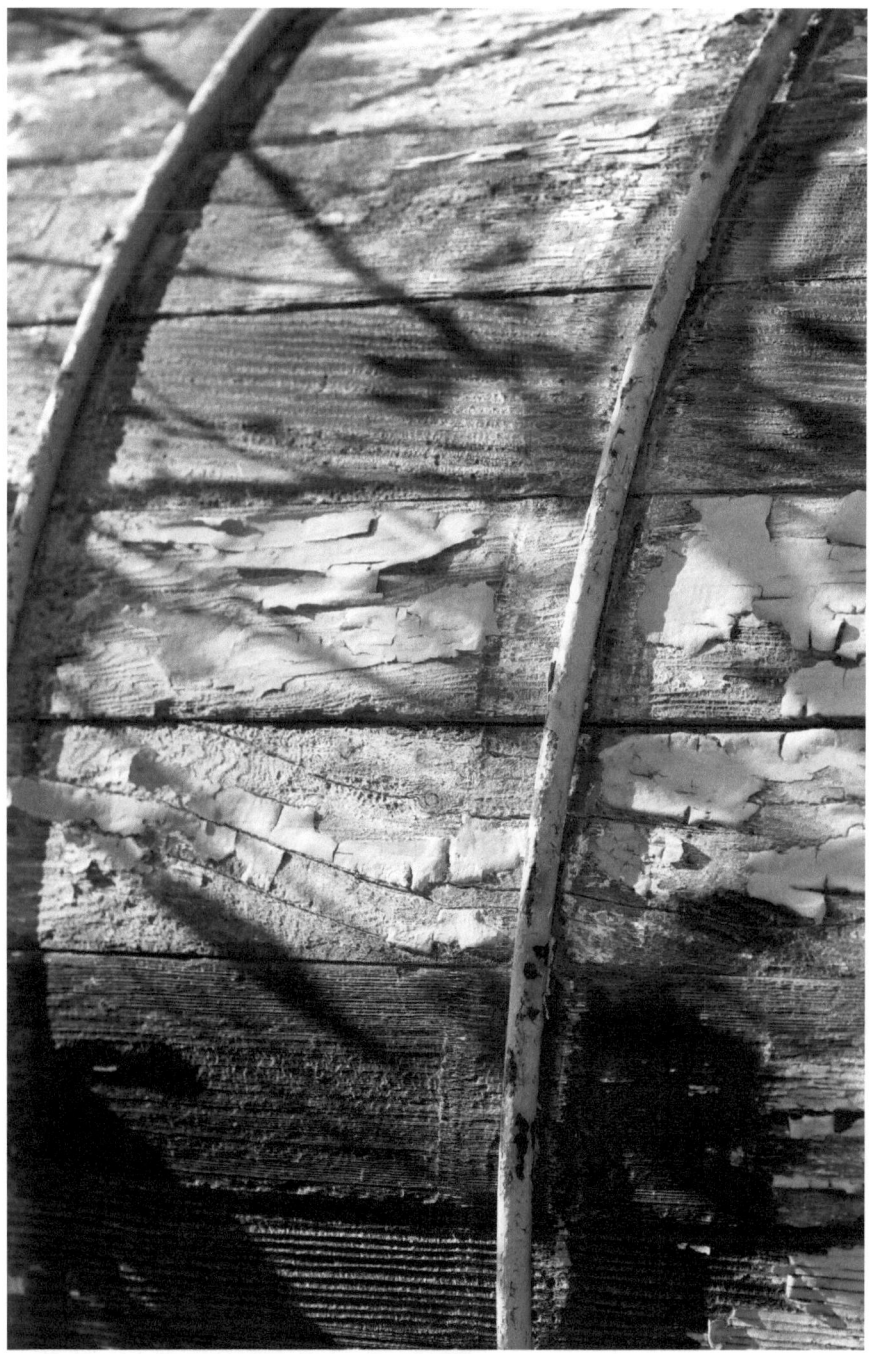

1608

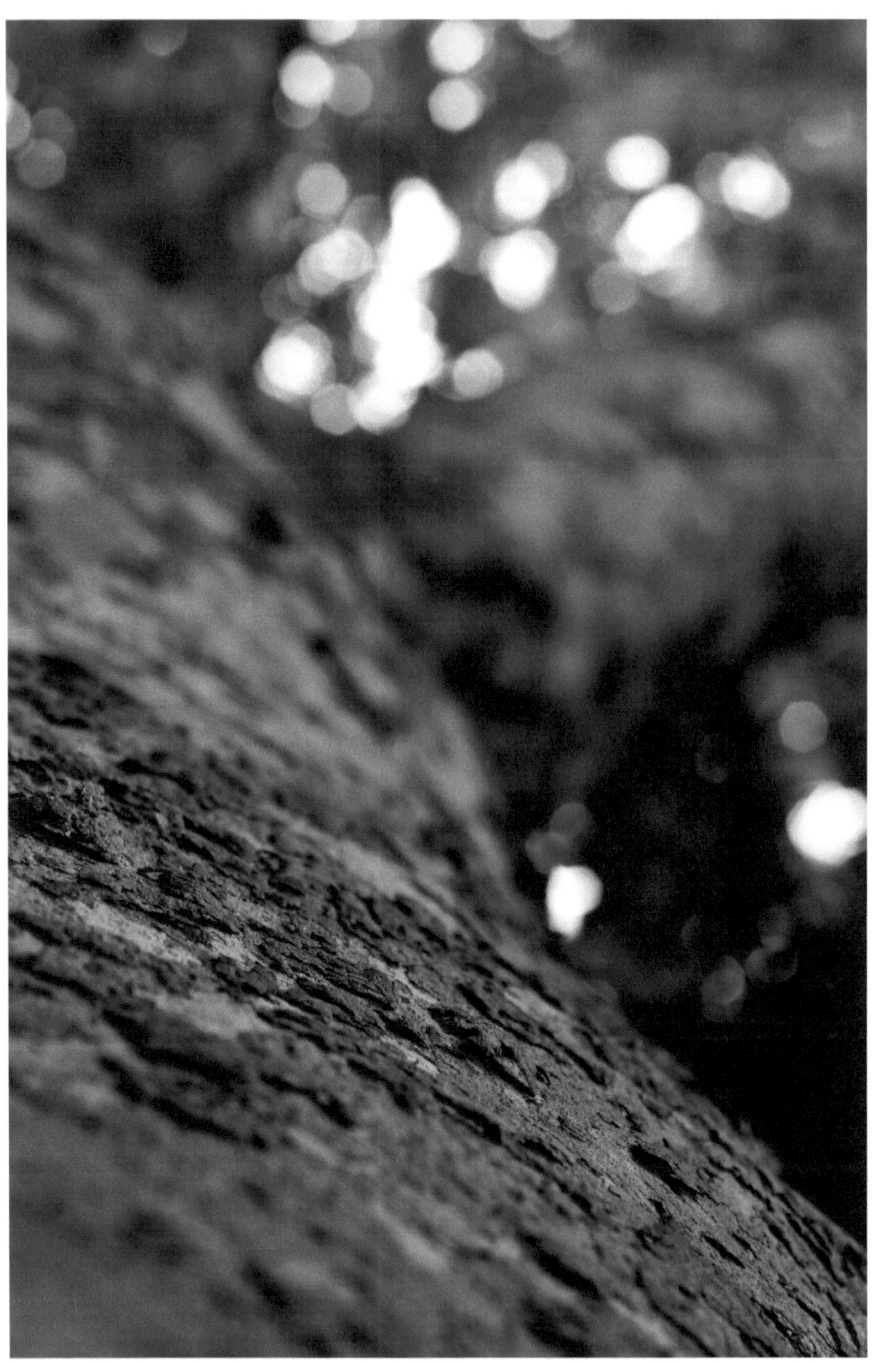

2068

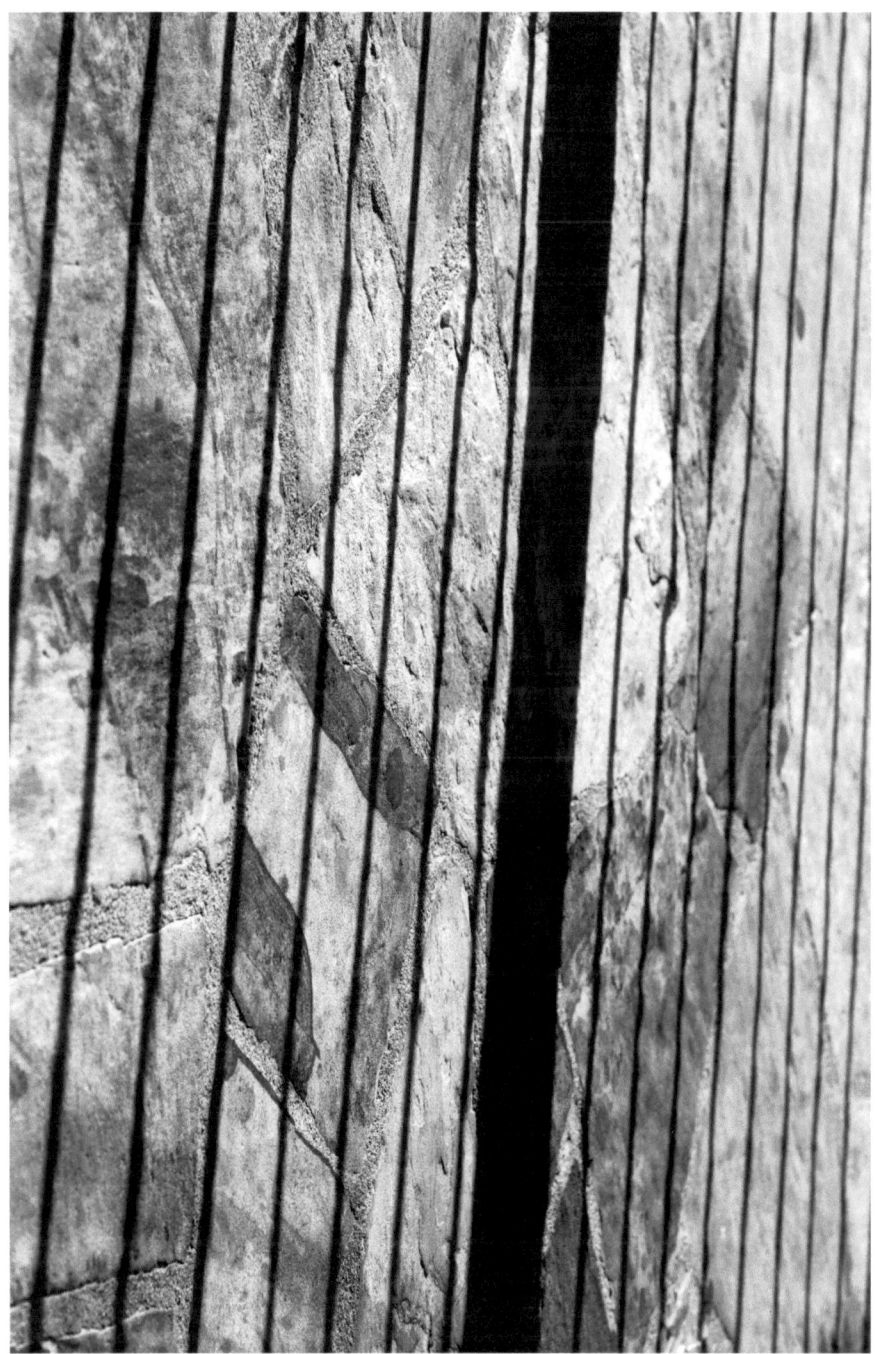

2089

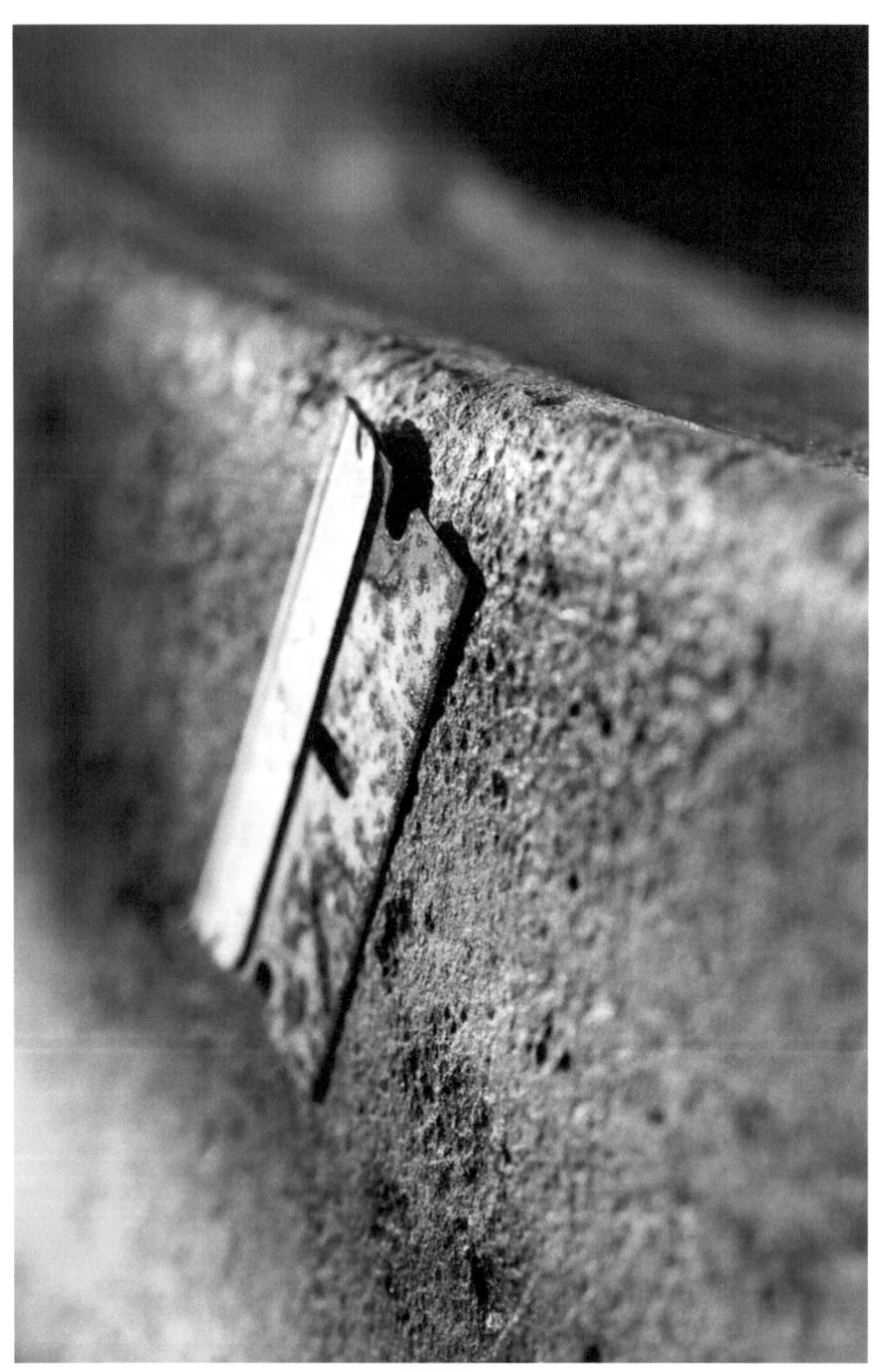

2467

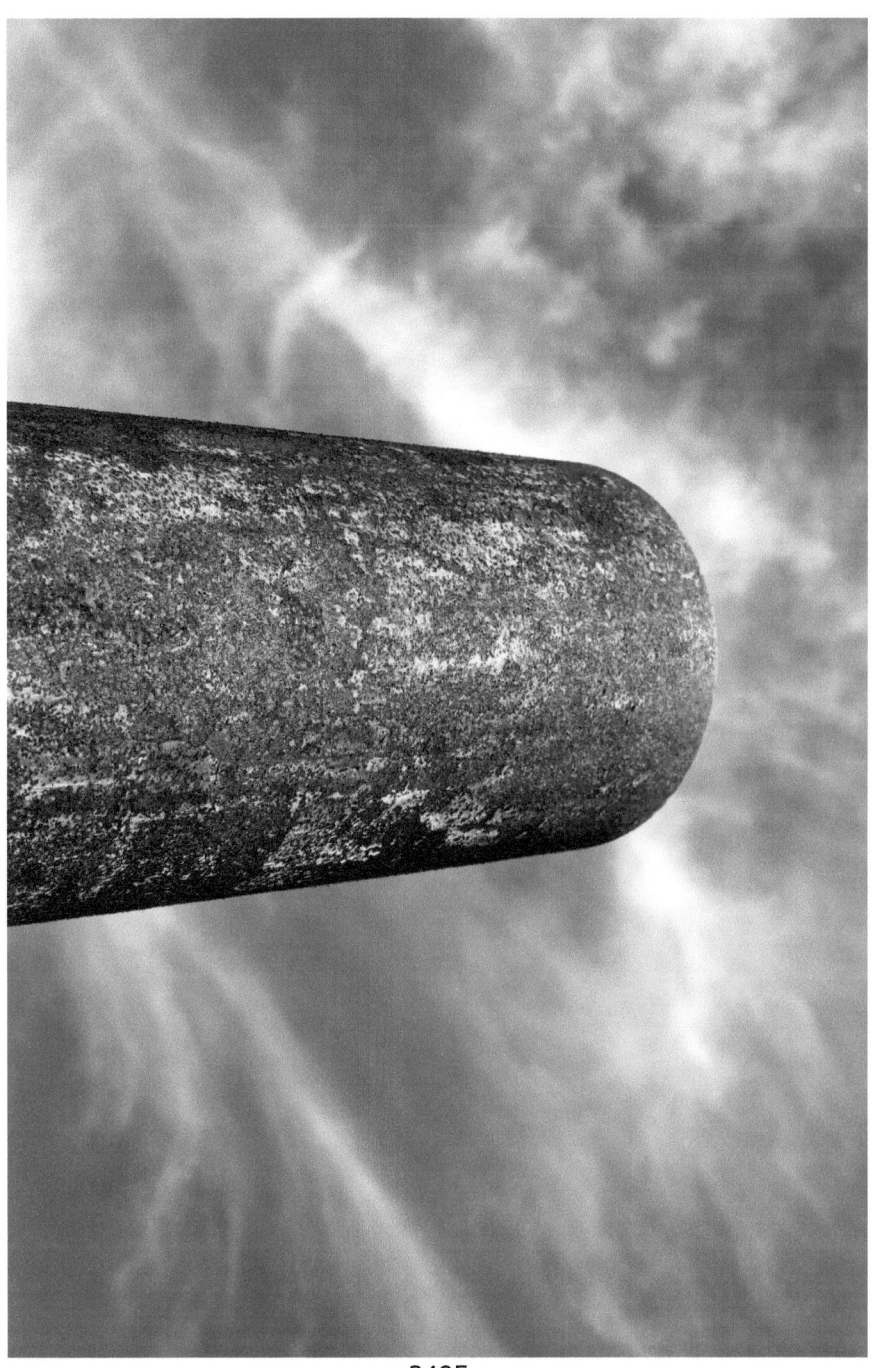

2495

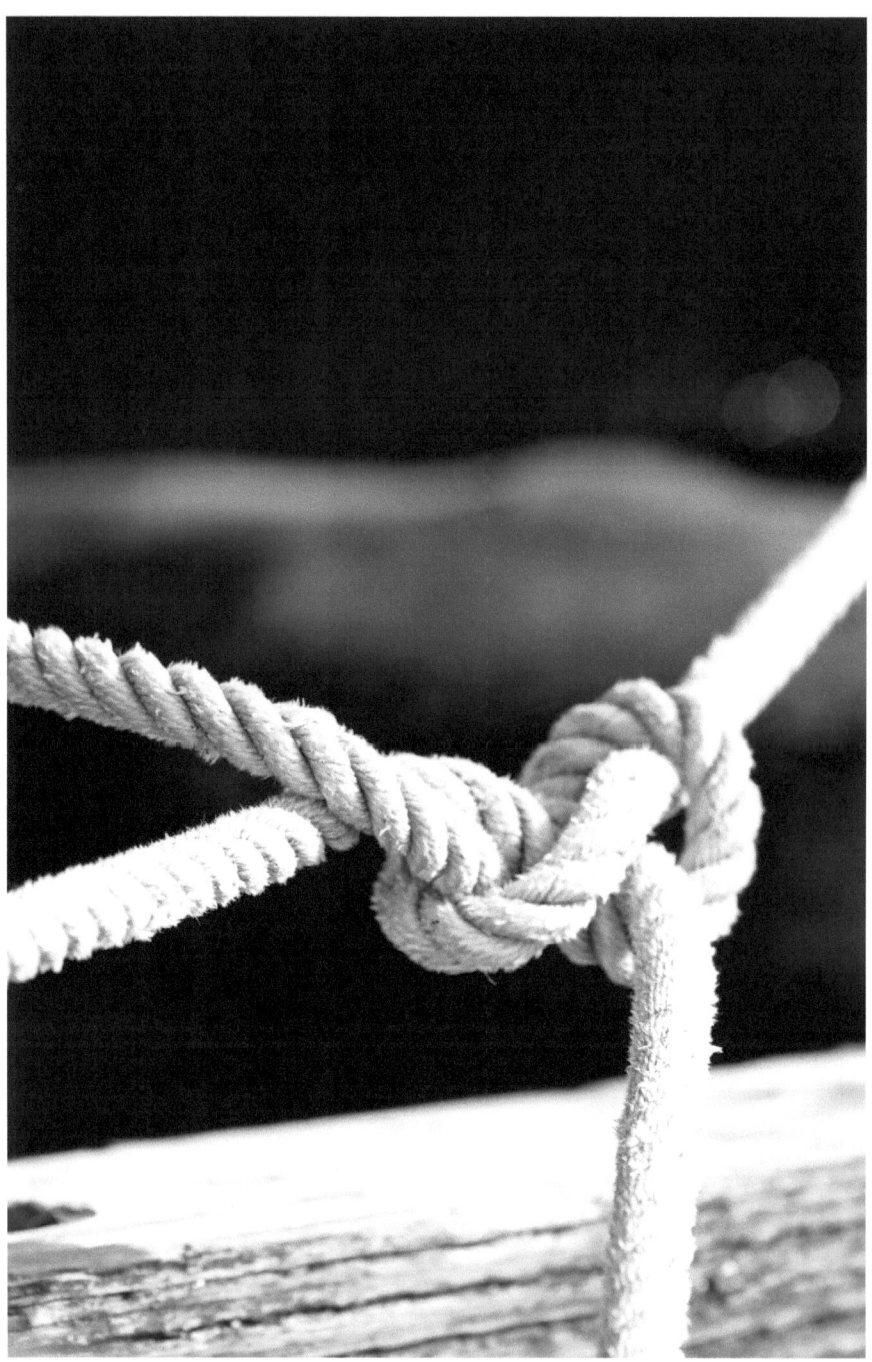

2686

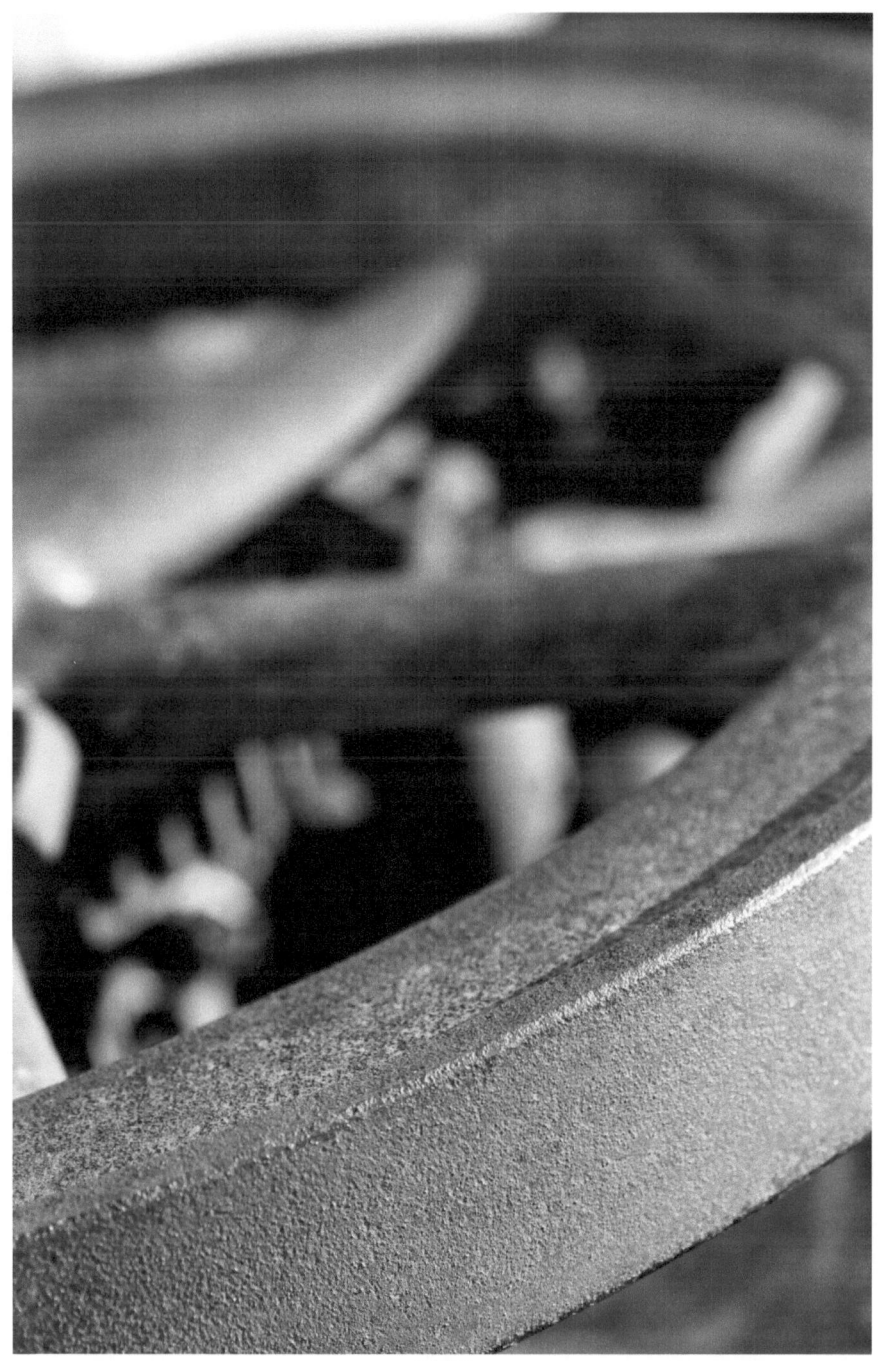

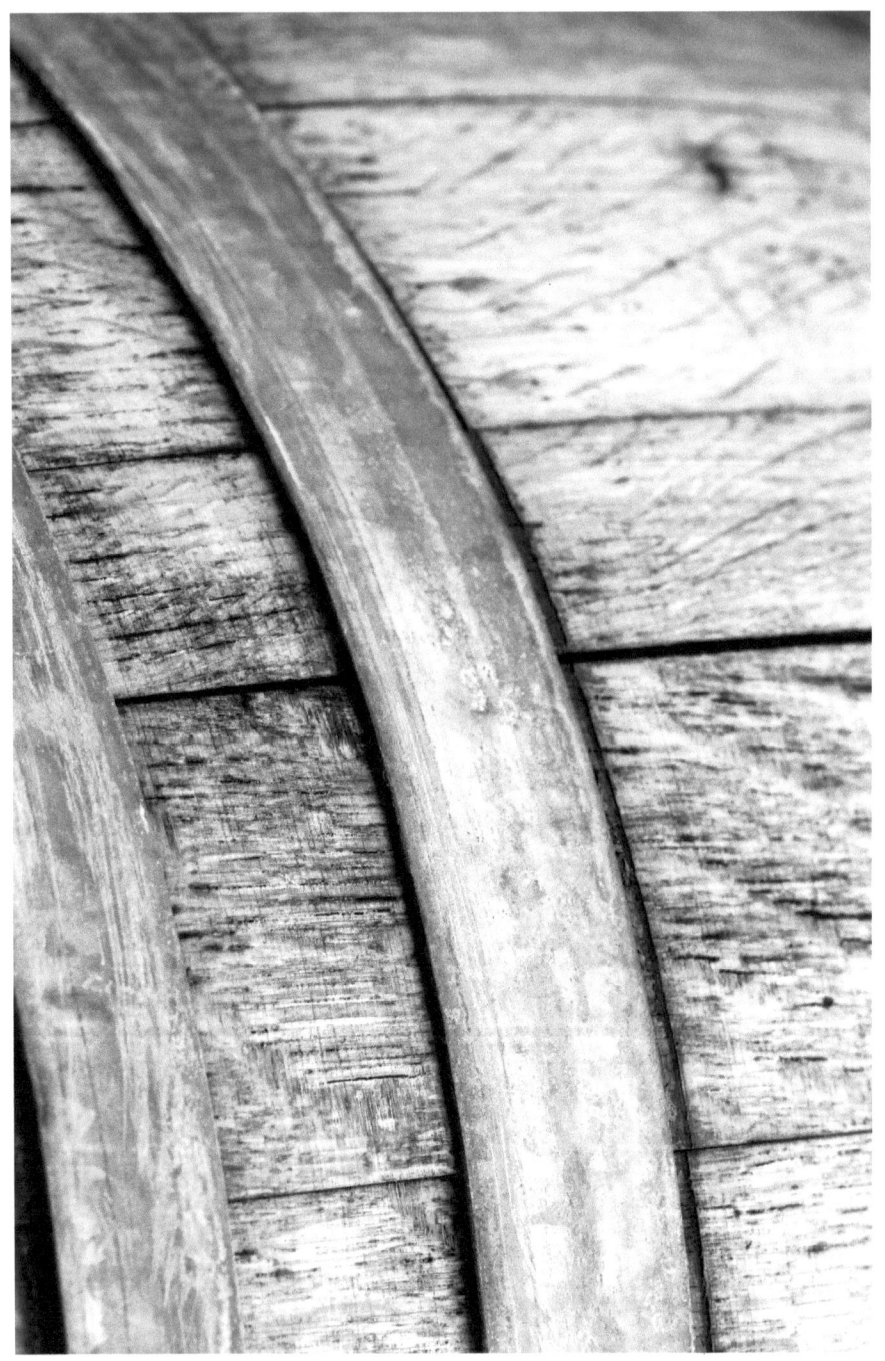

3151

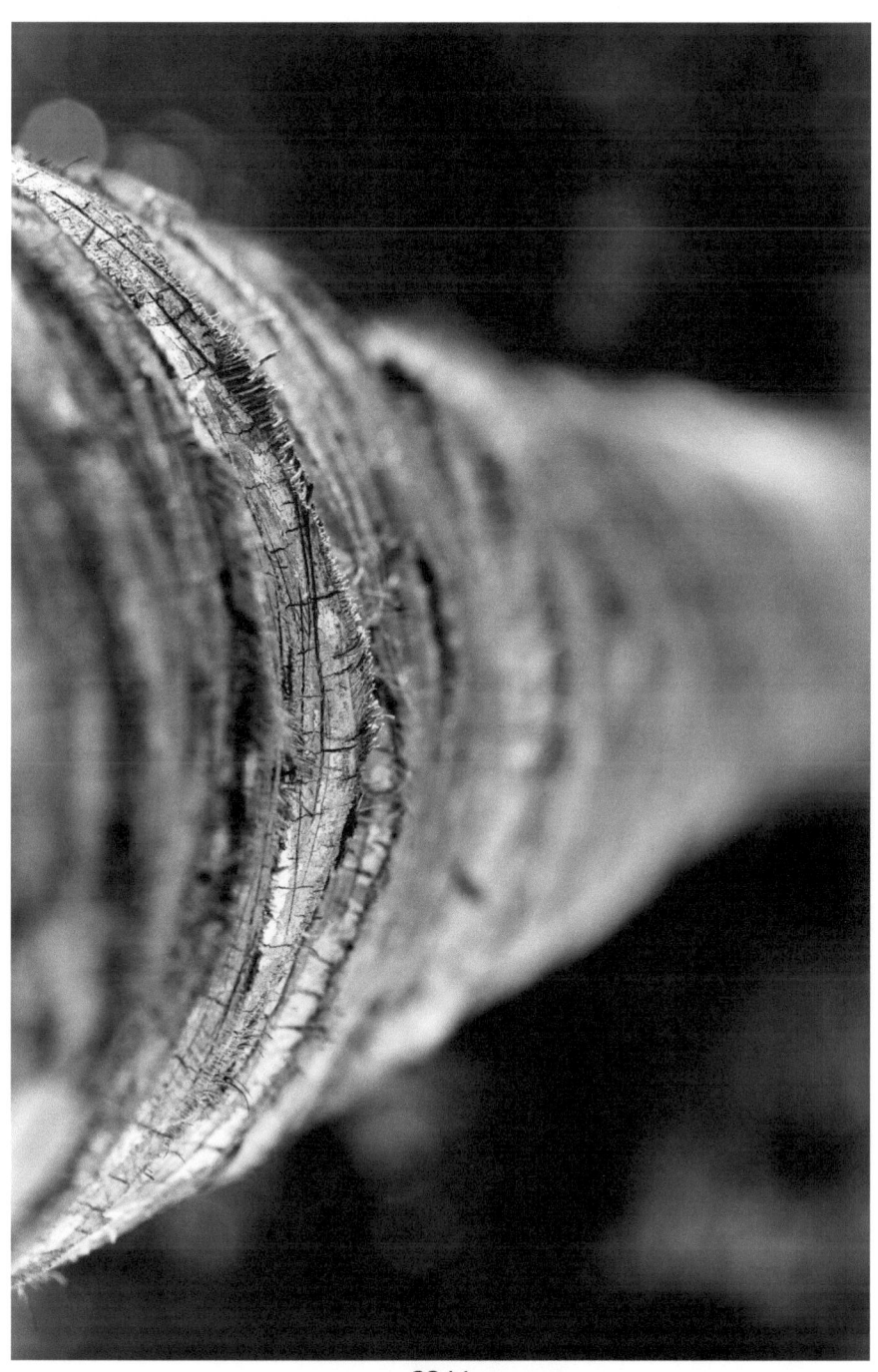

3244

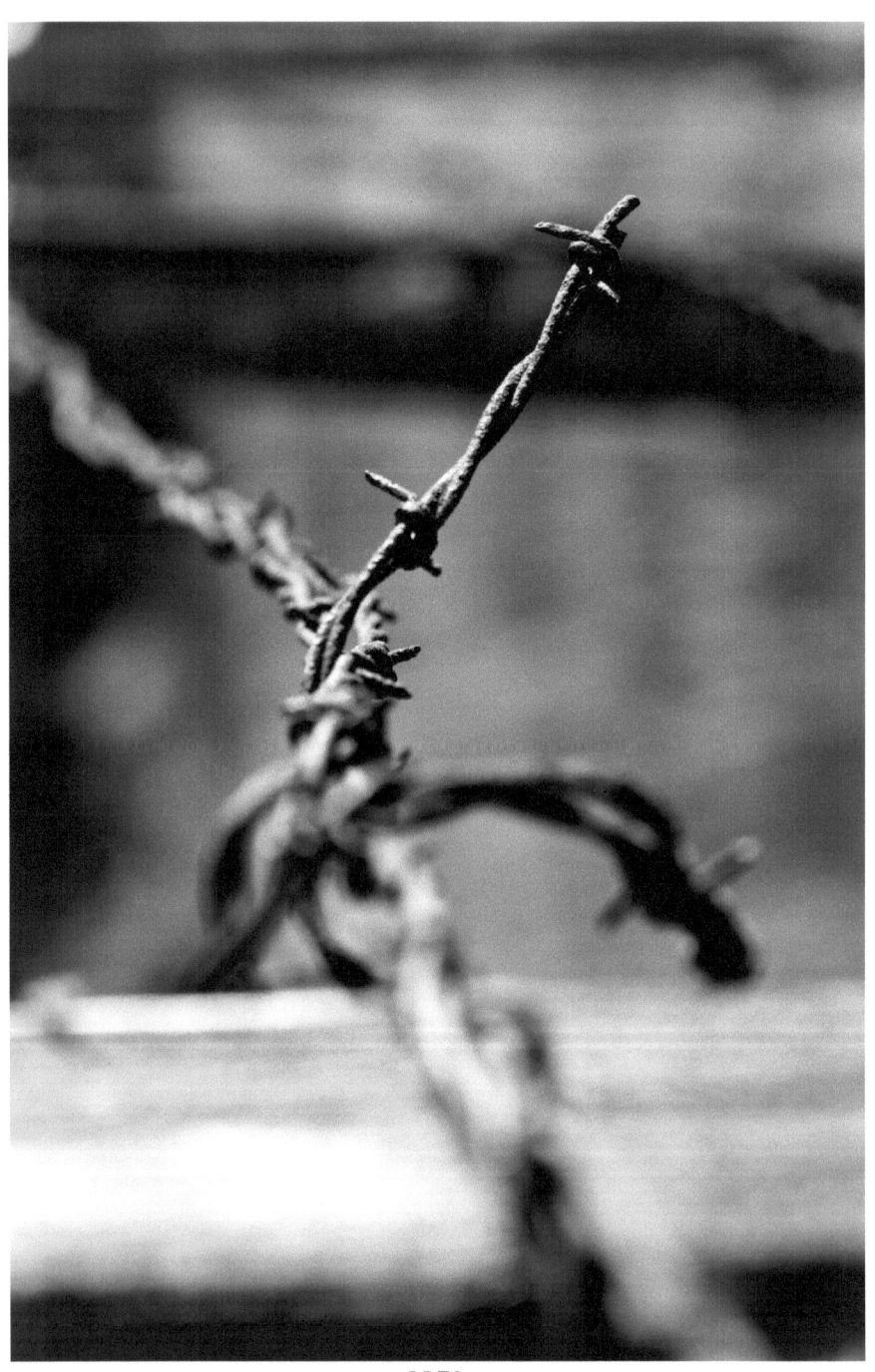

3359

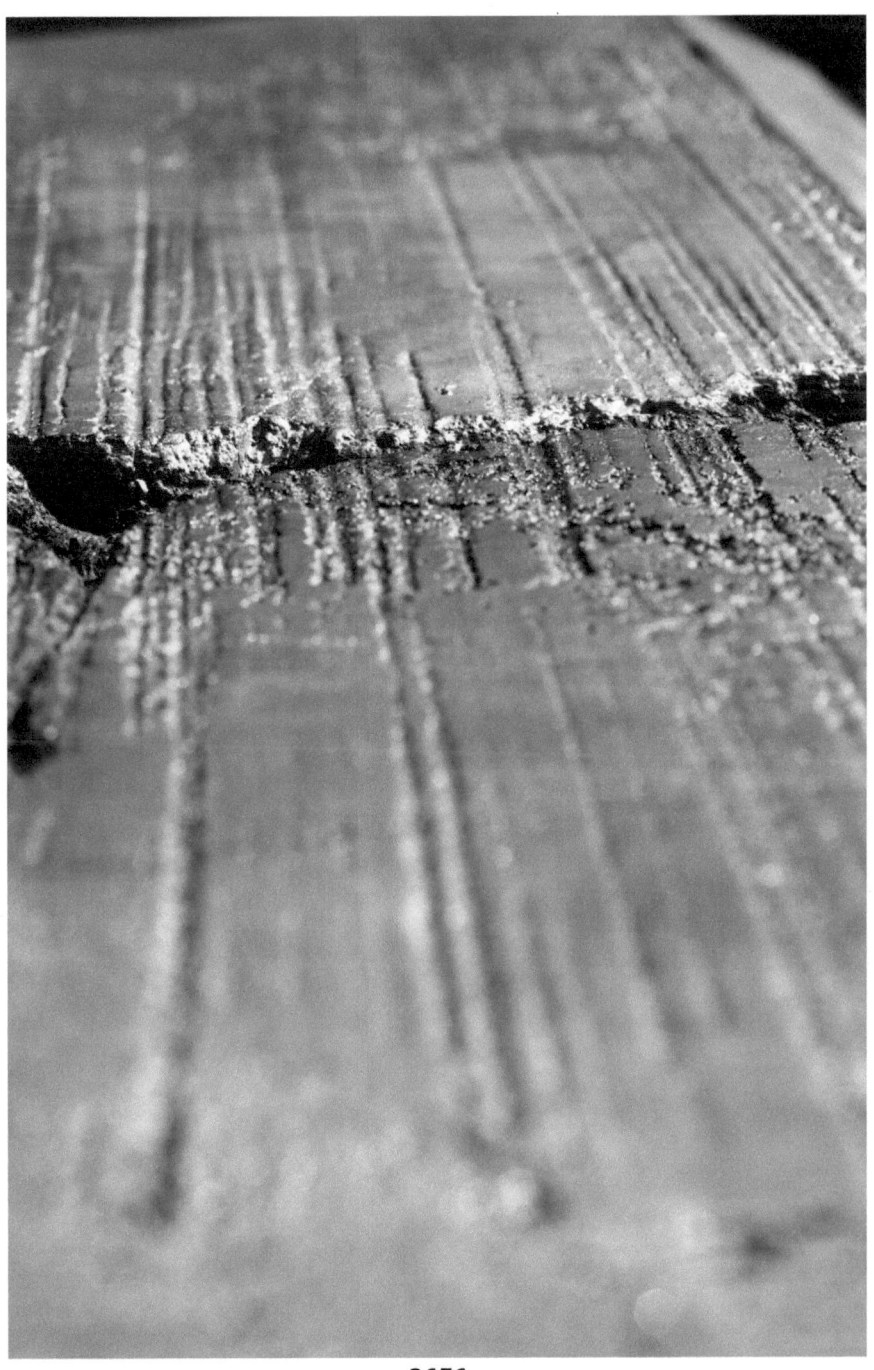

3656

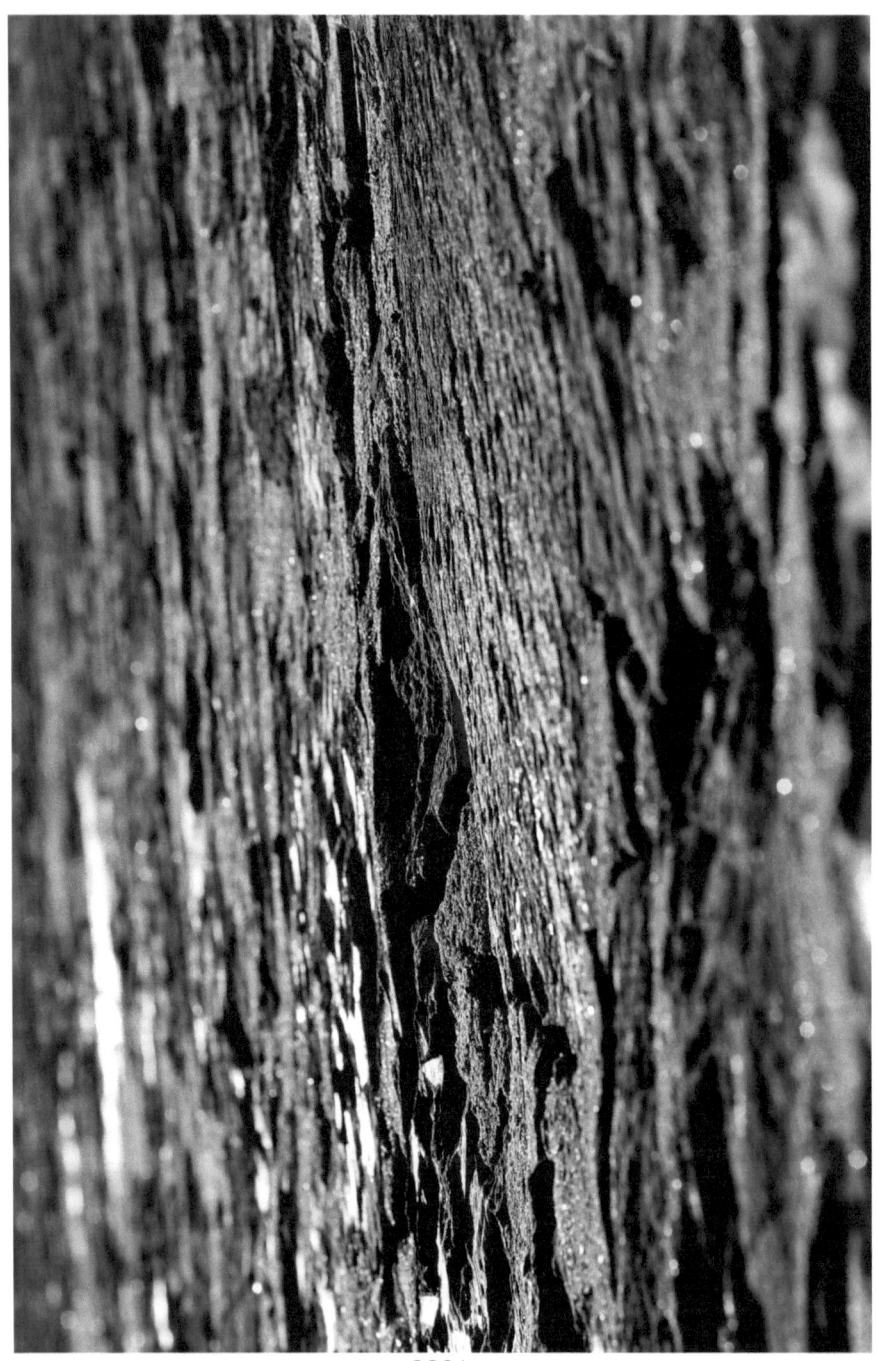

3881

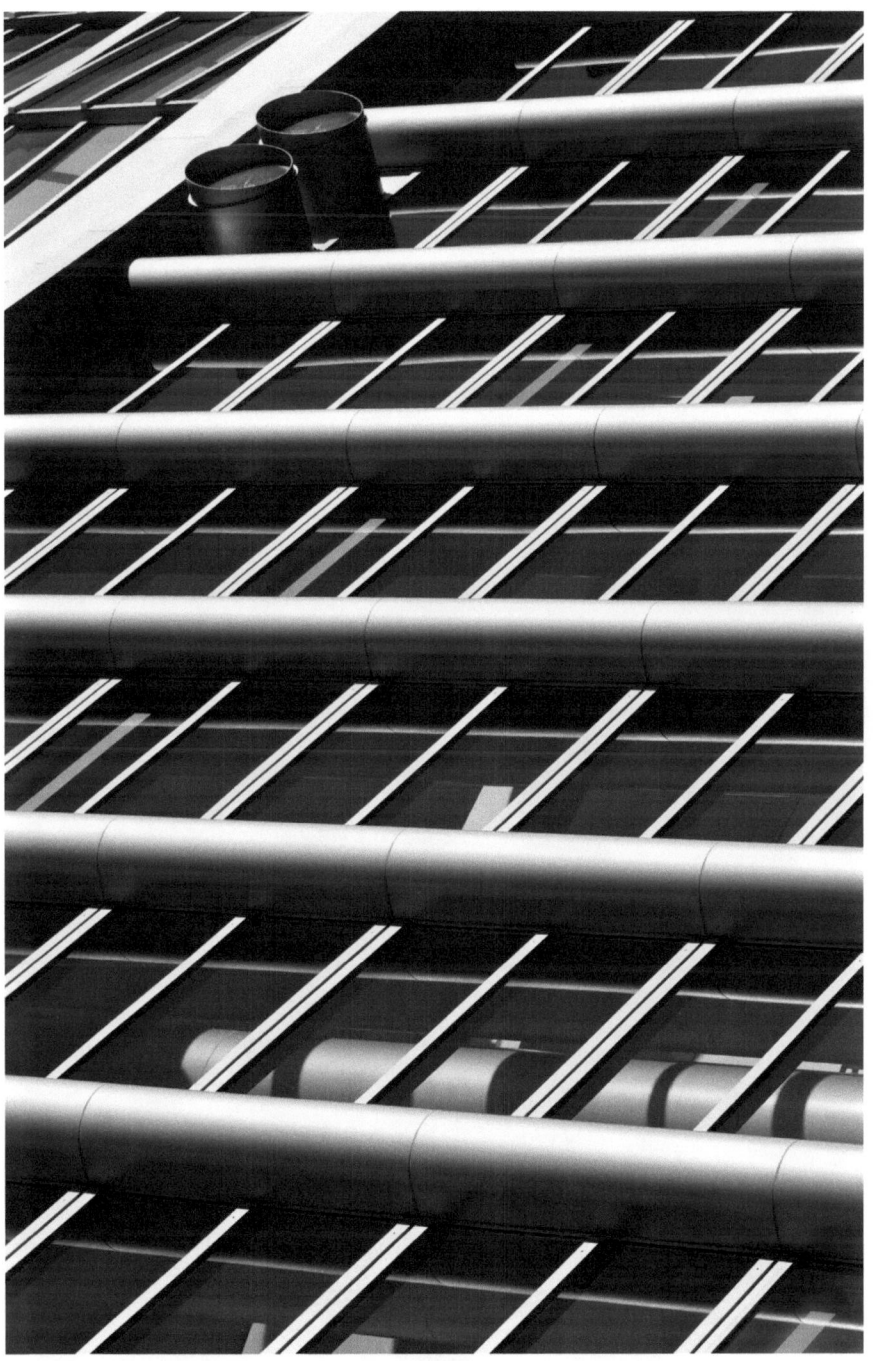

3943

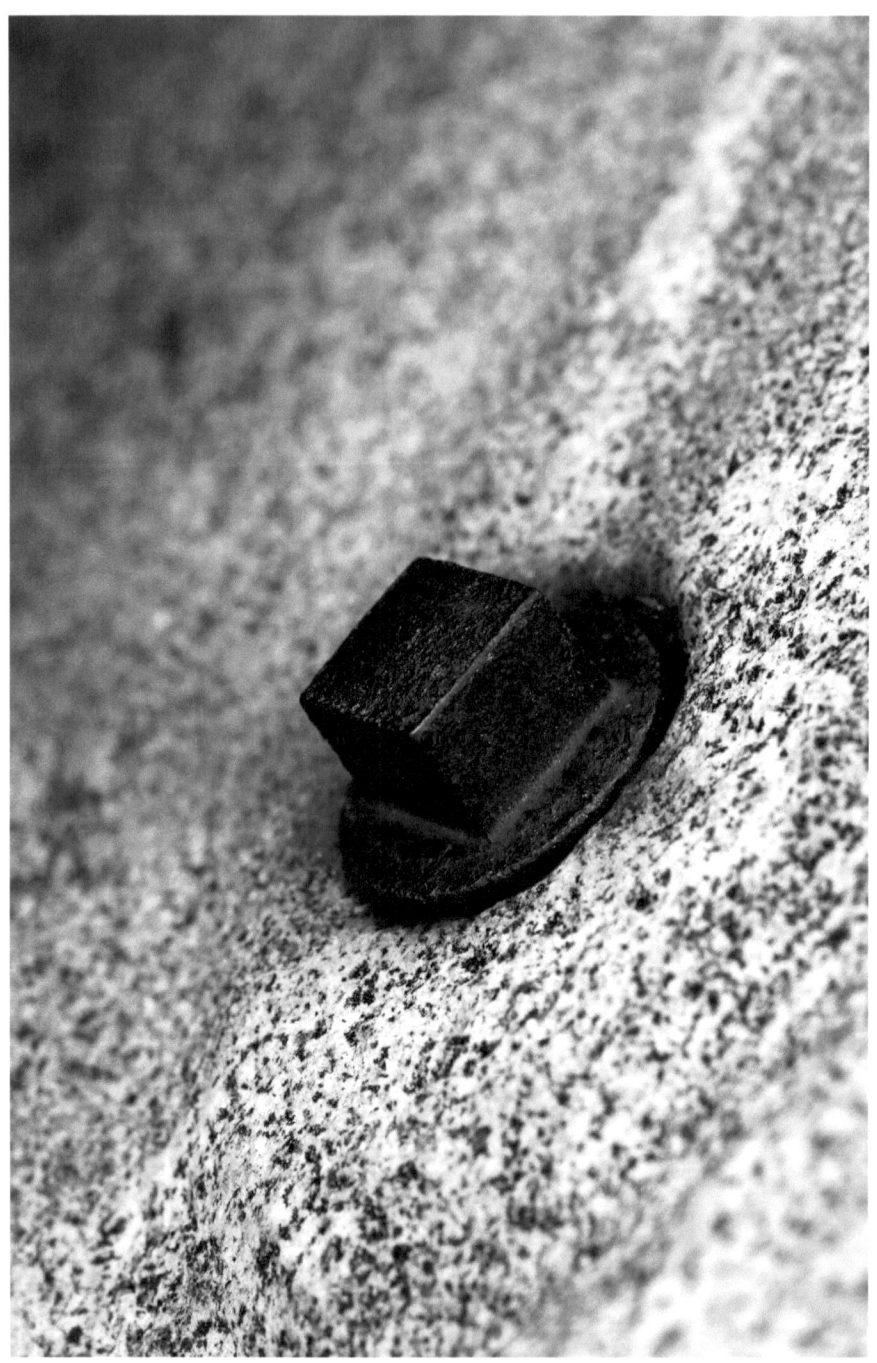

4035

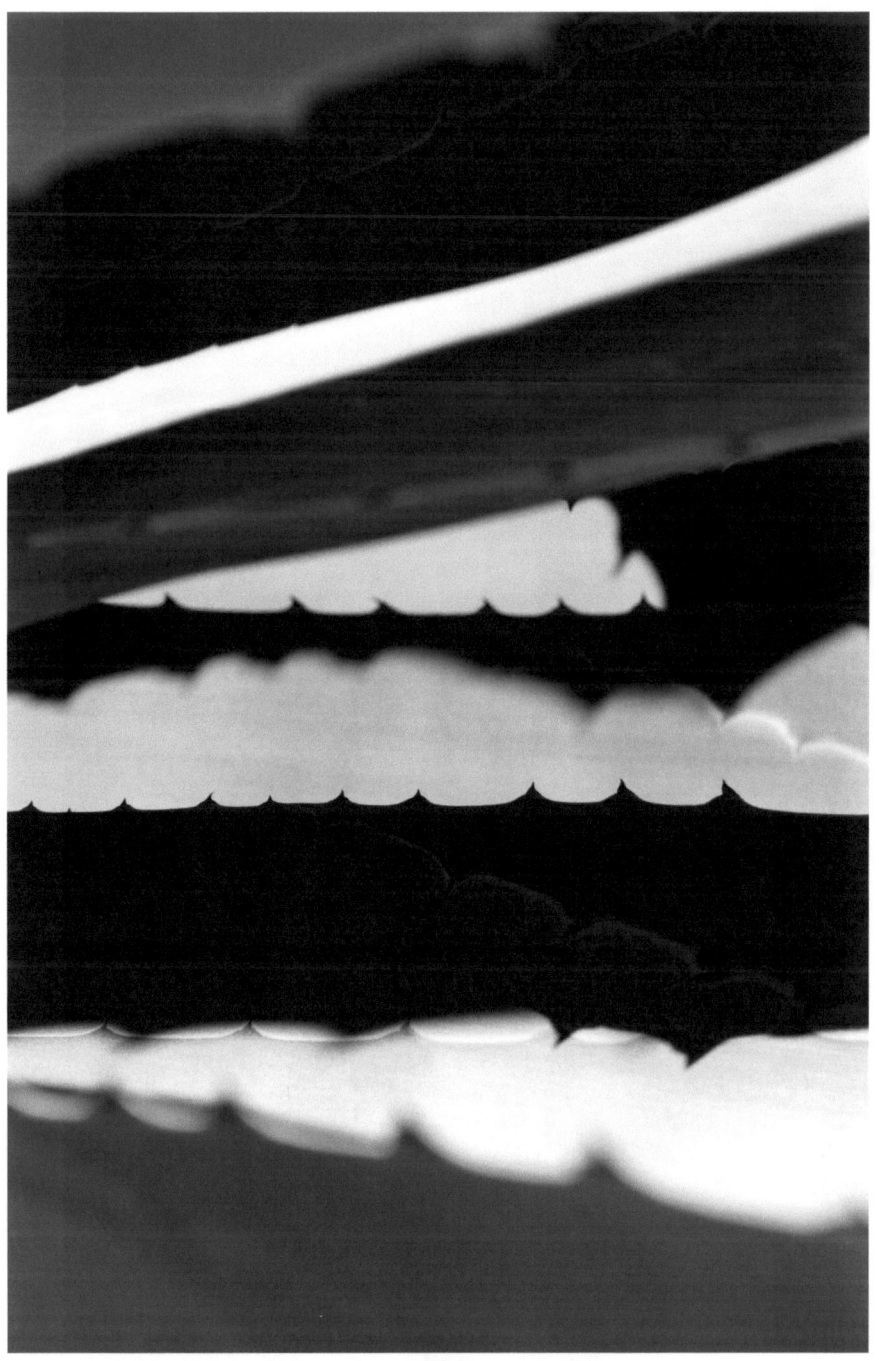

4099

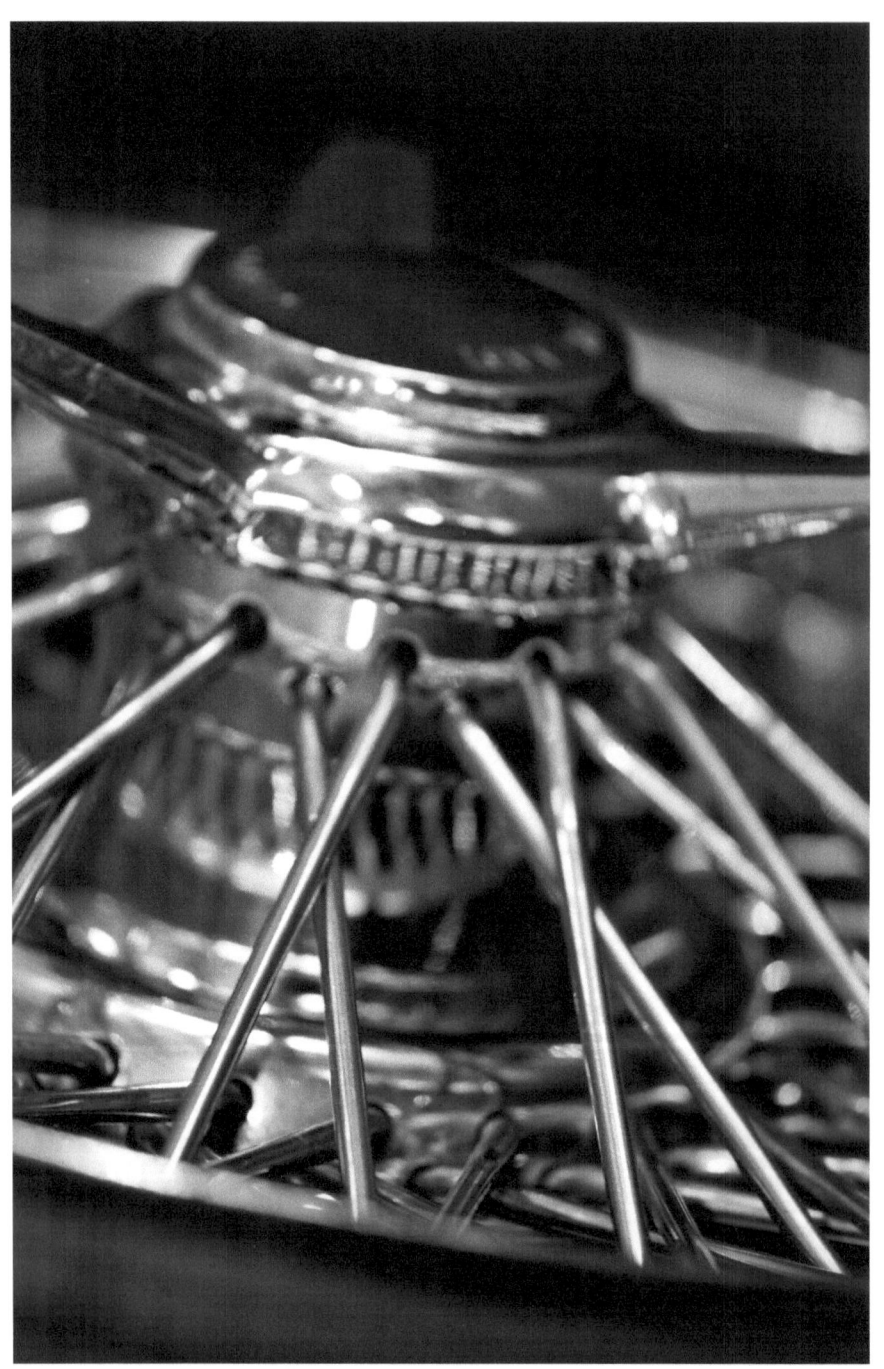

4193

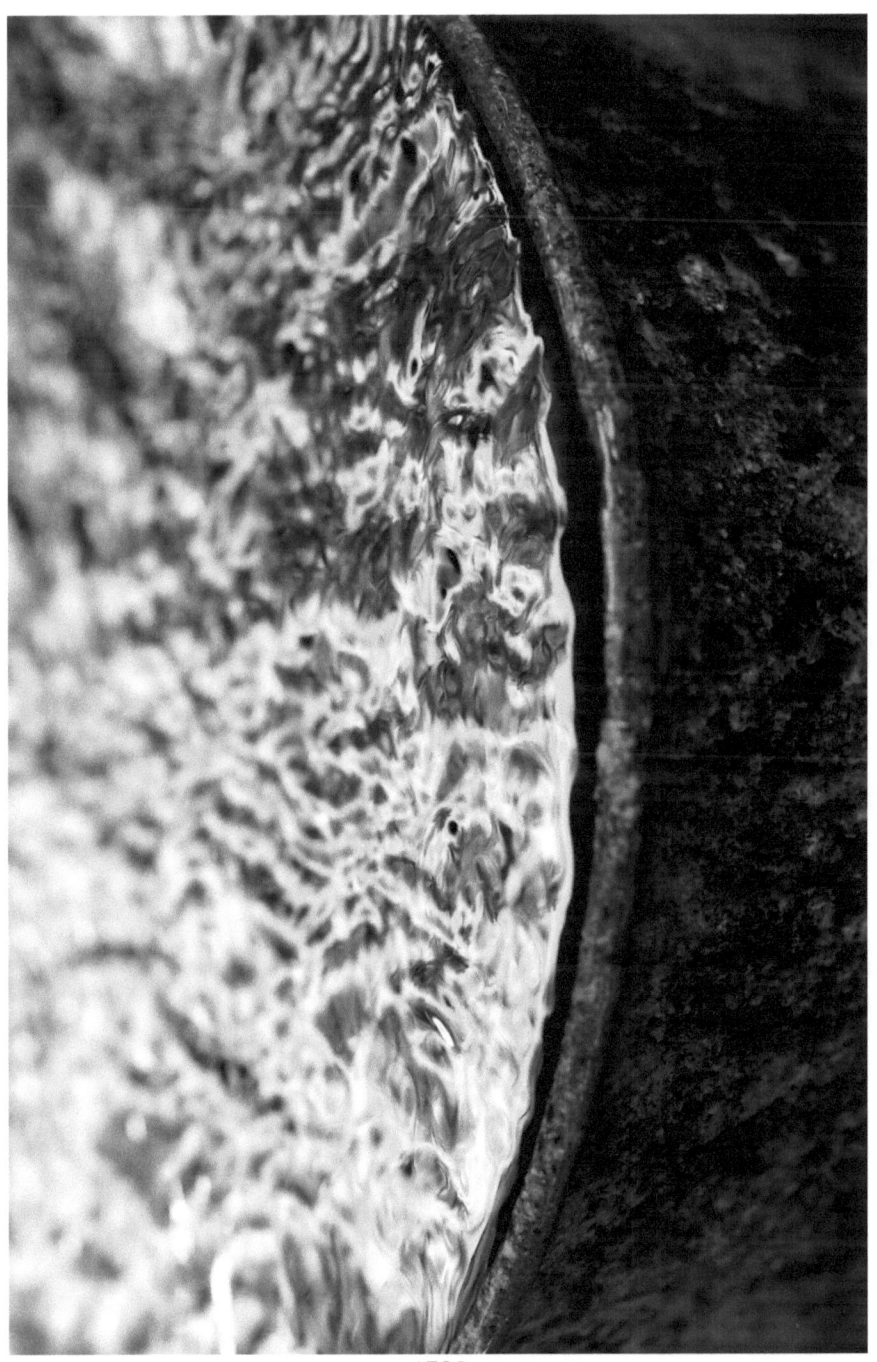

4533

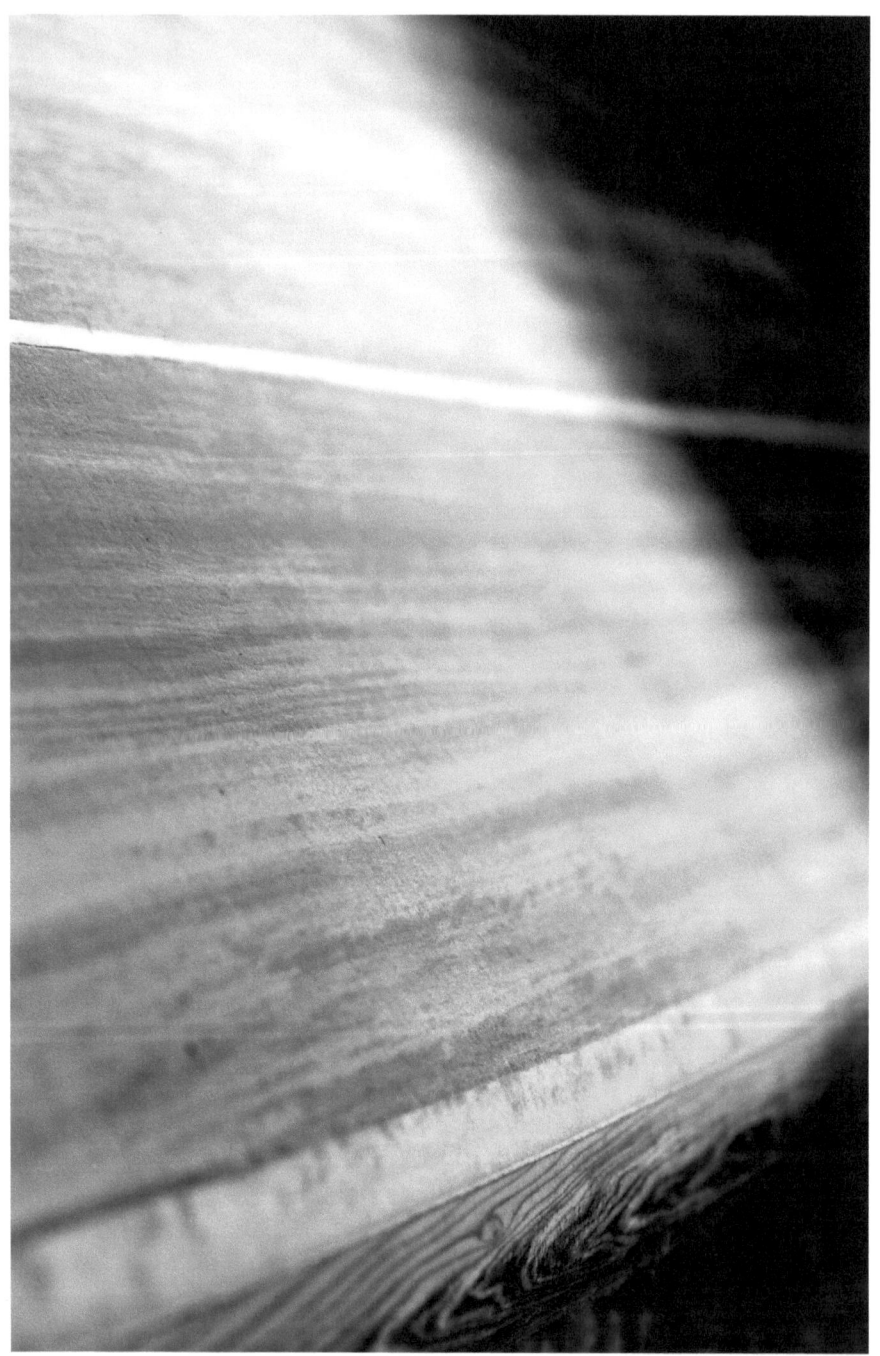

5171

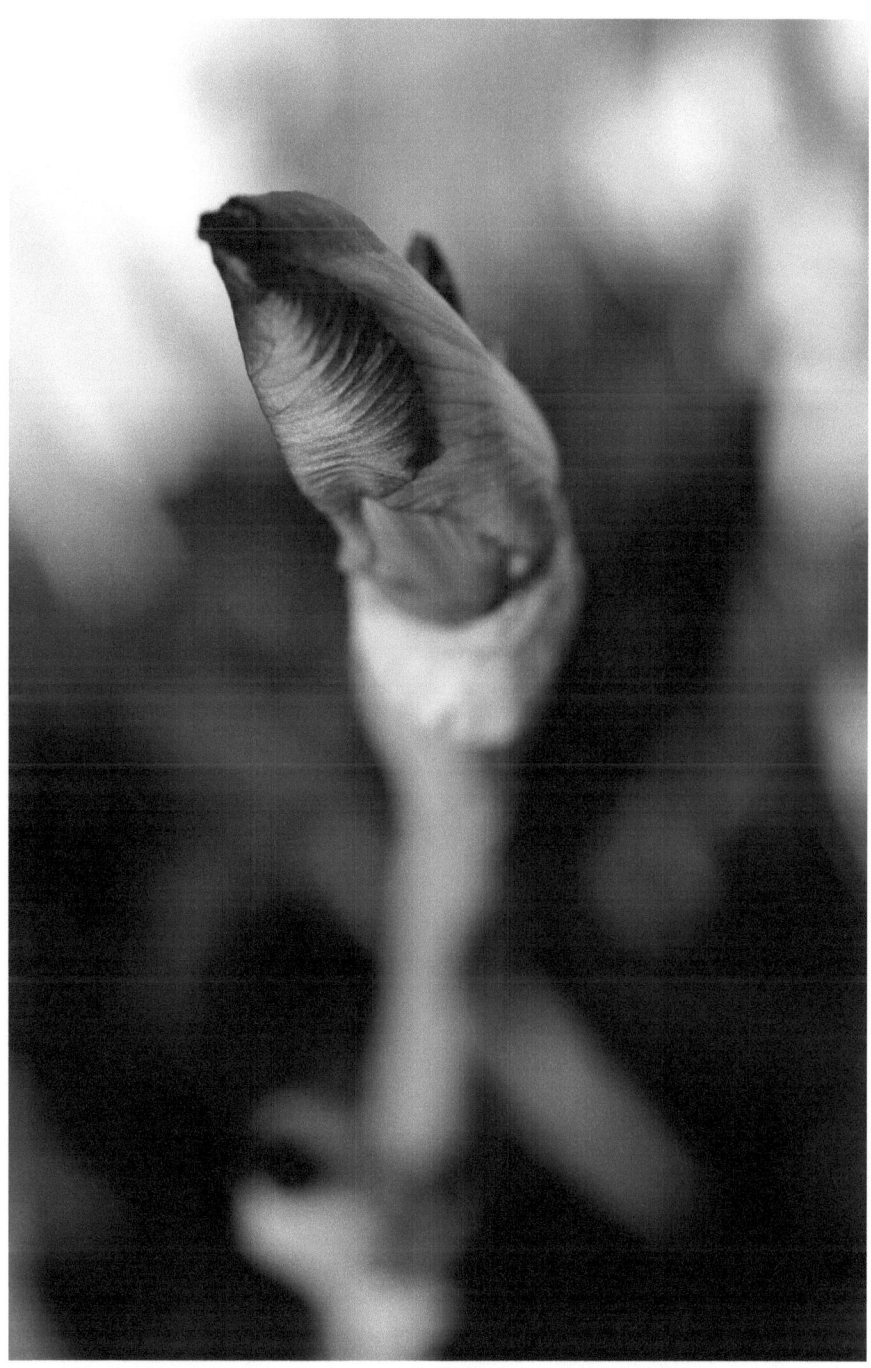

5492

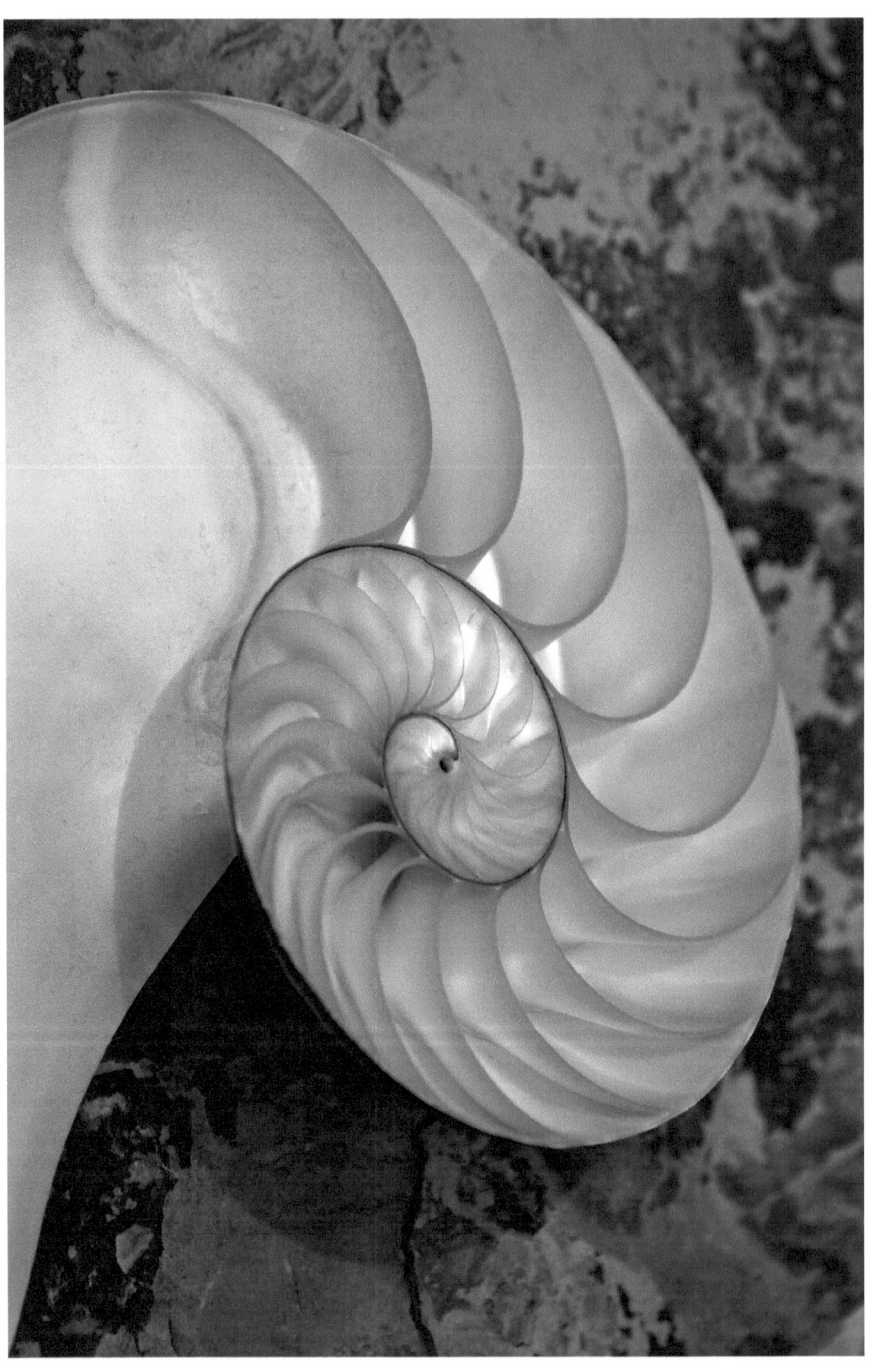

5708

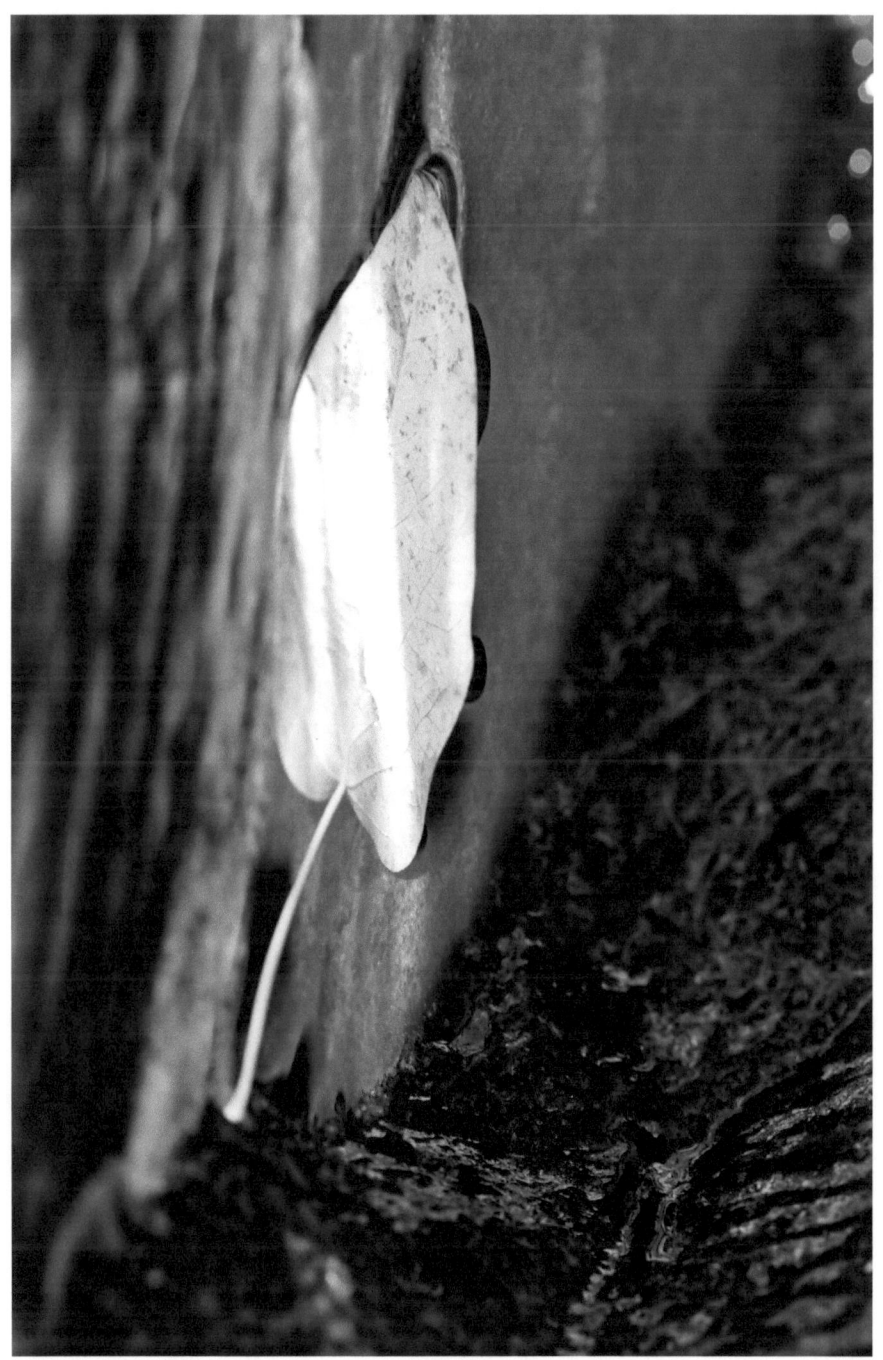

5750

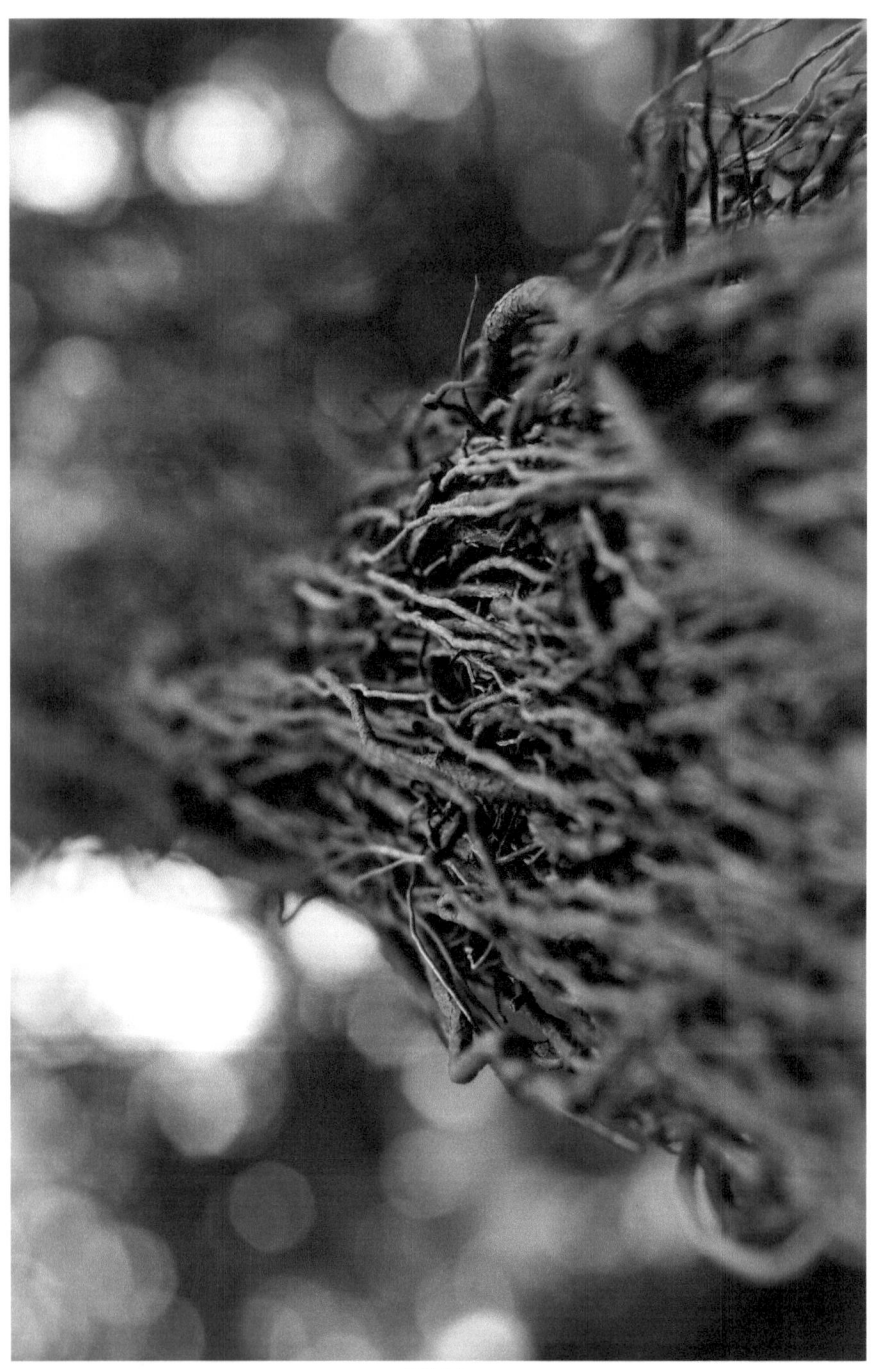

5811

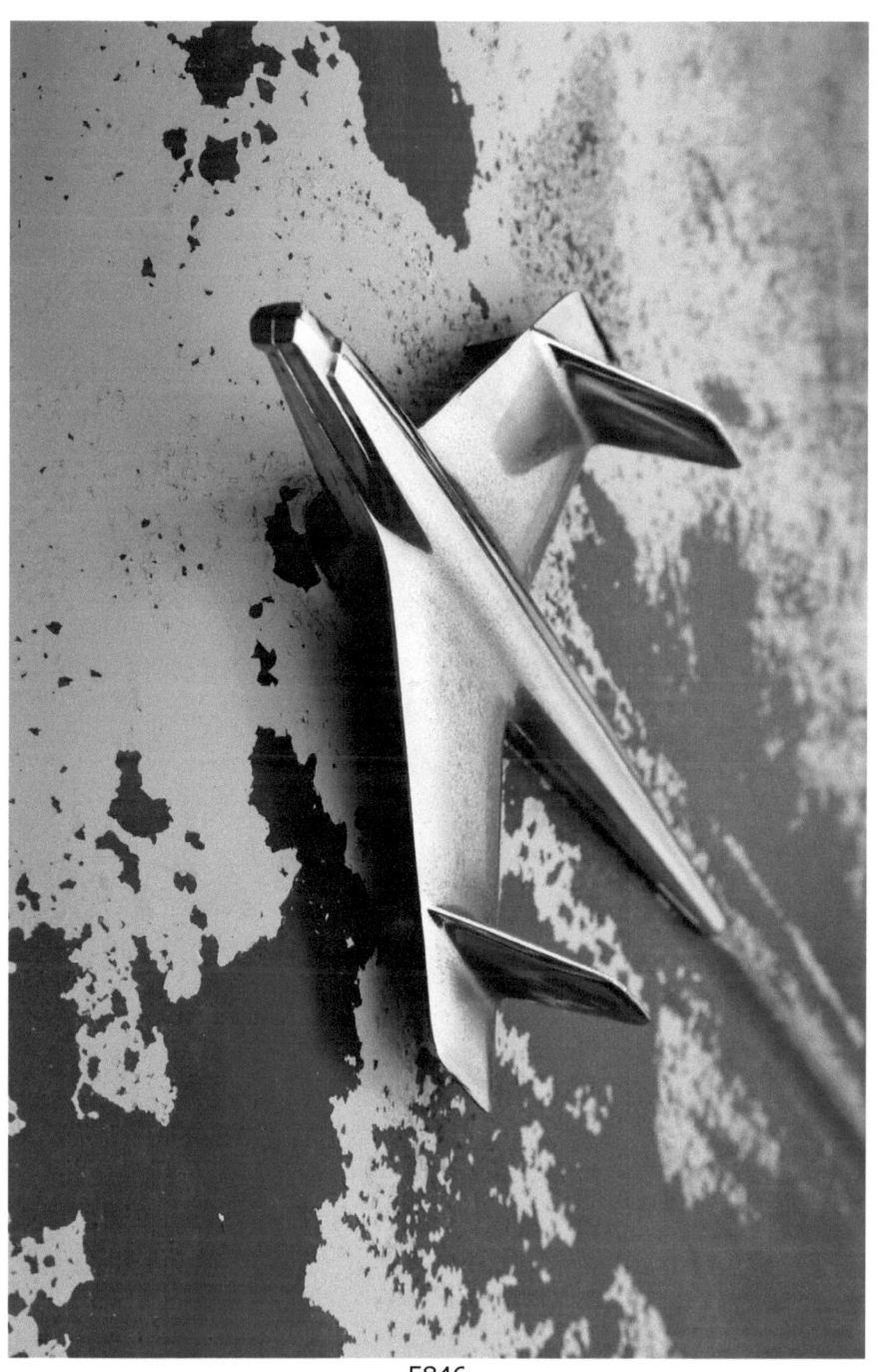

5846

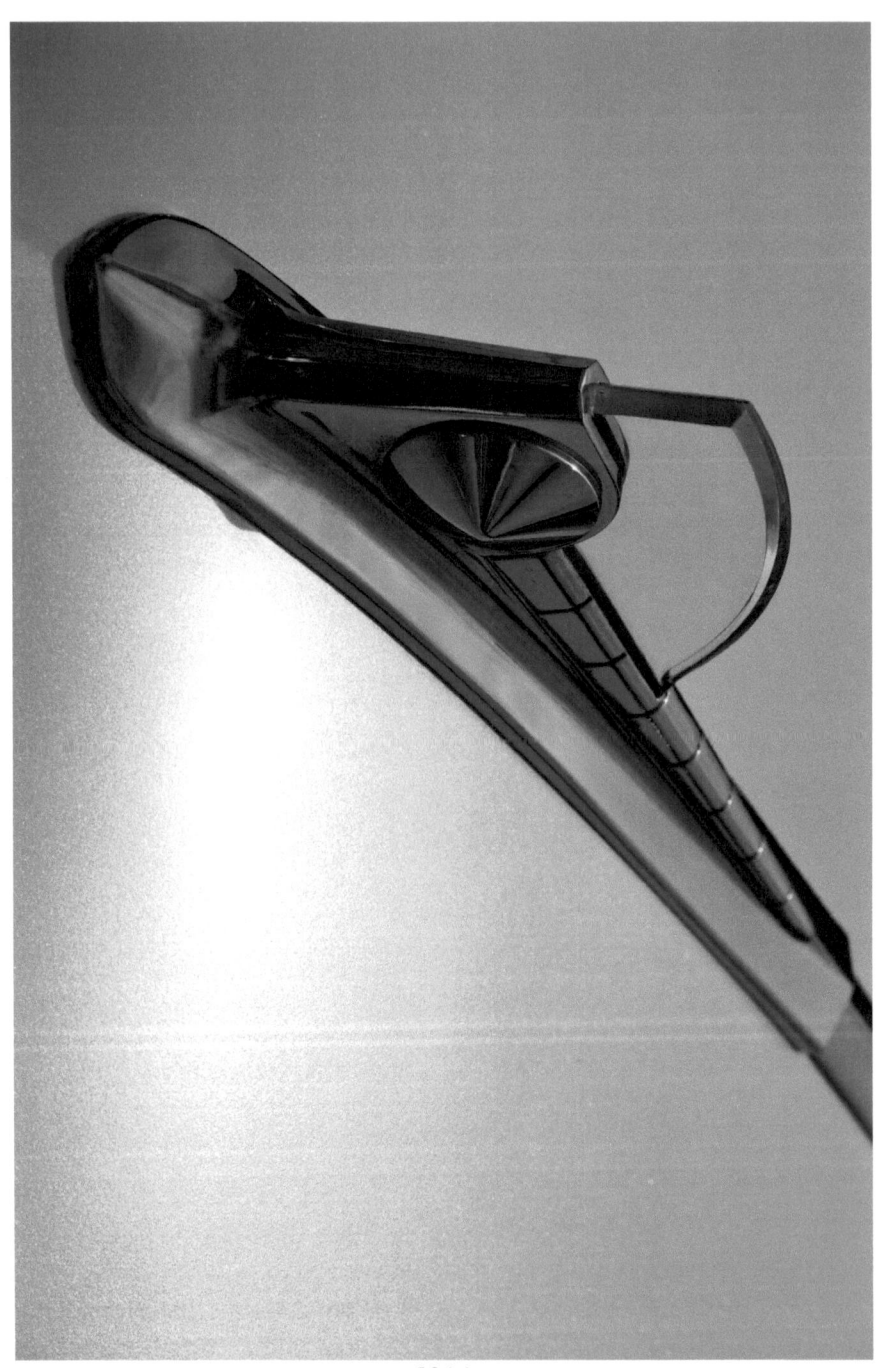

6014

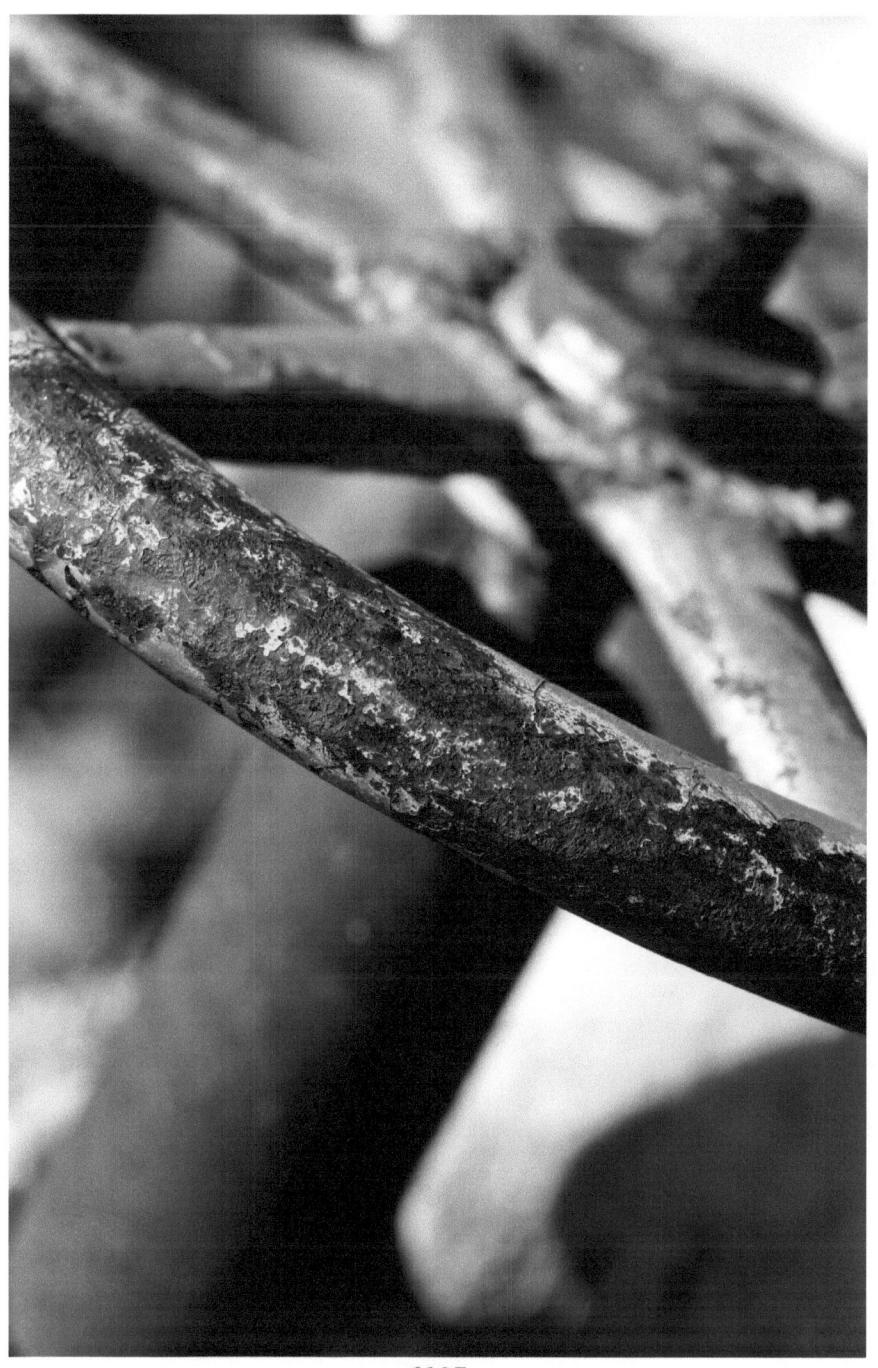

6095

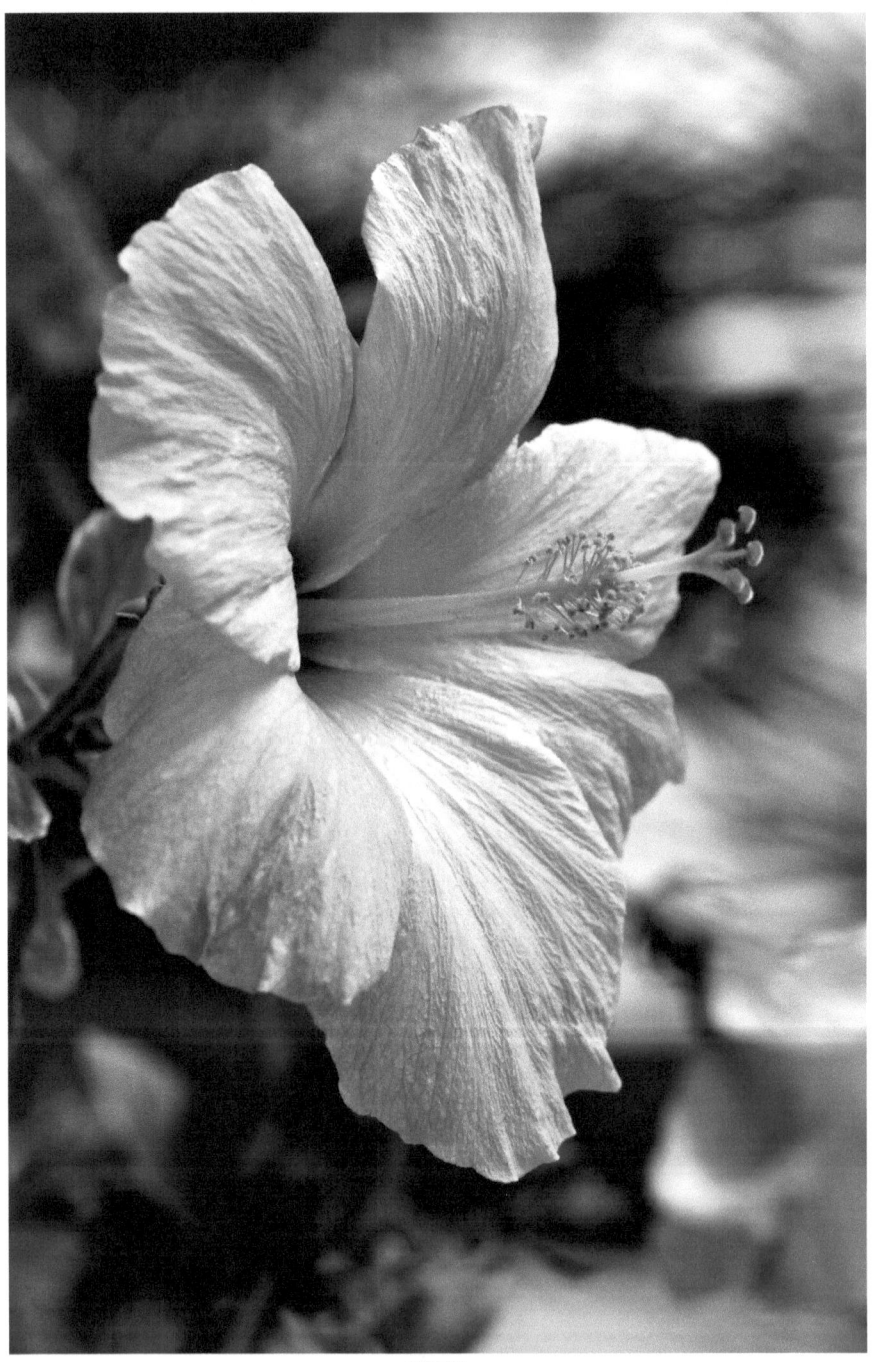

6990

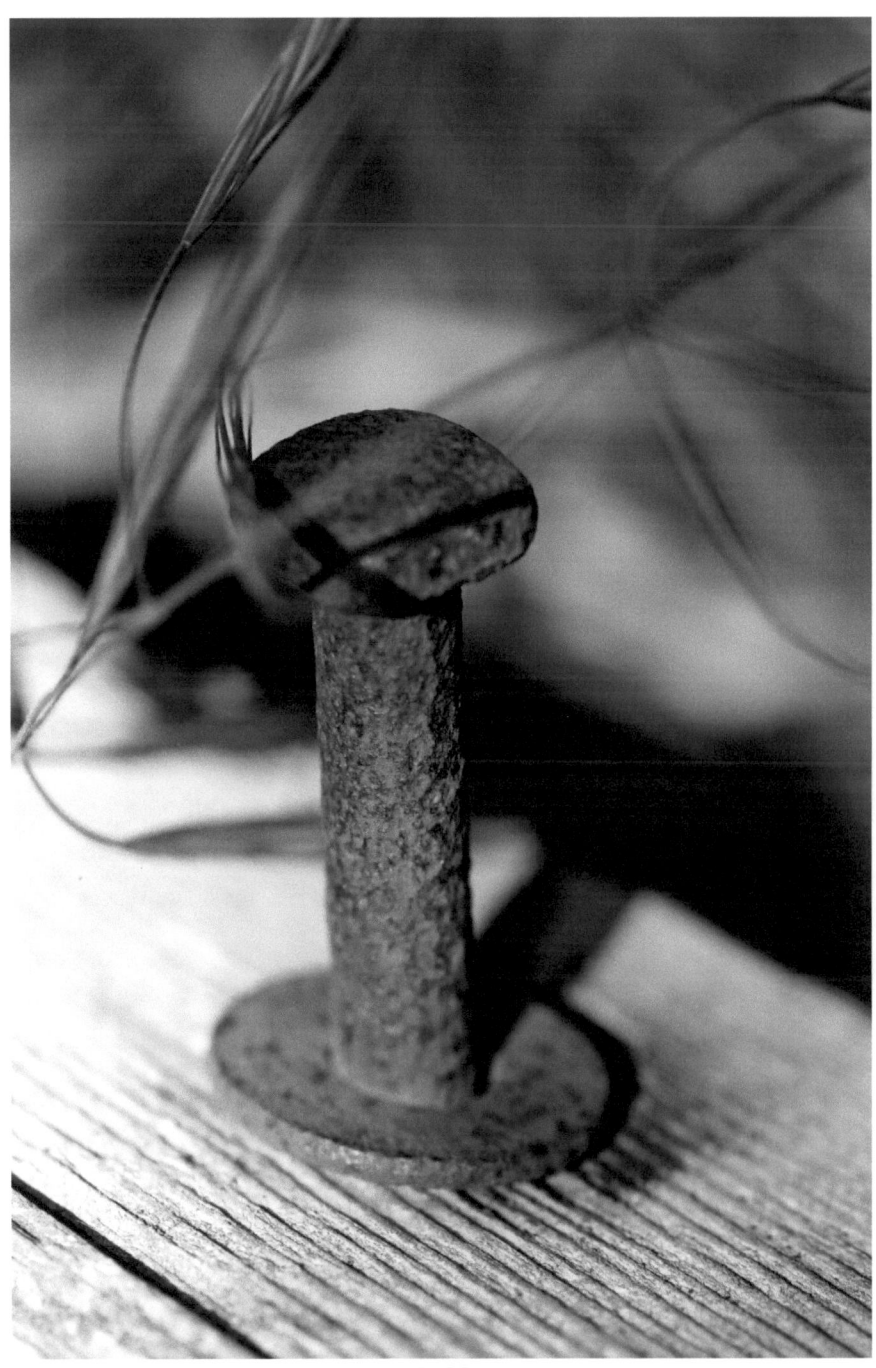

7182

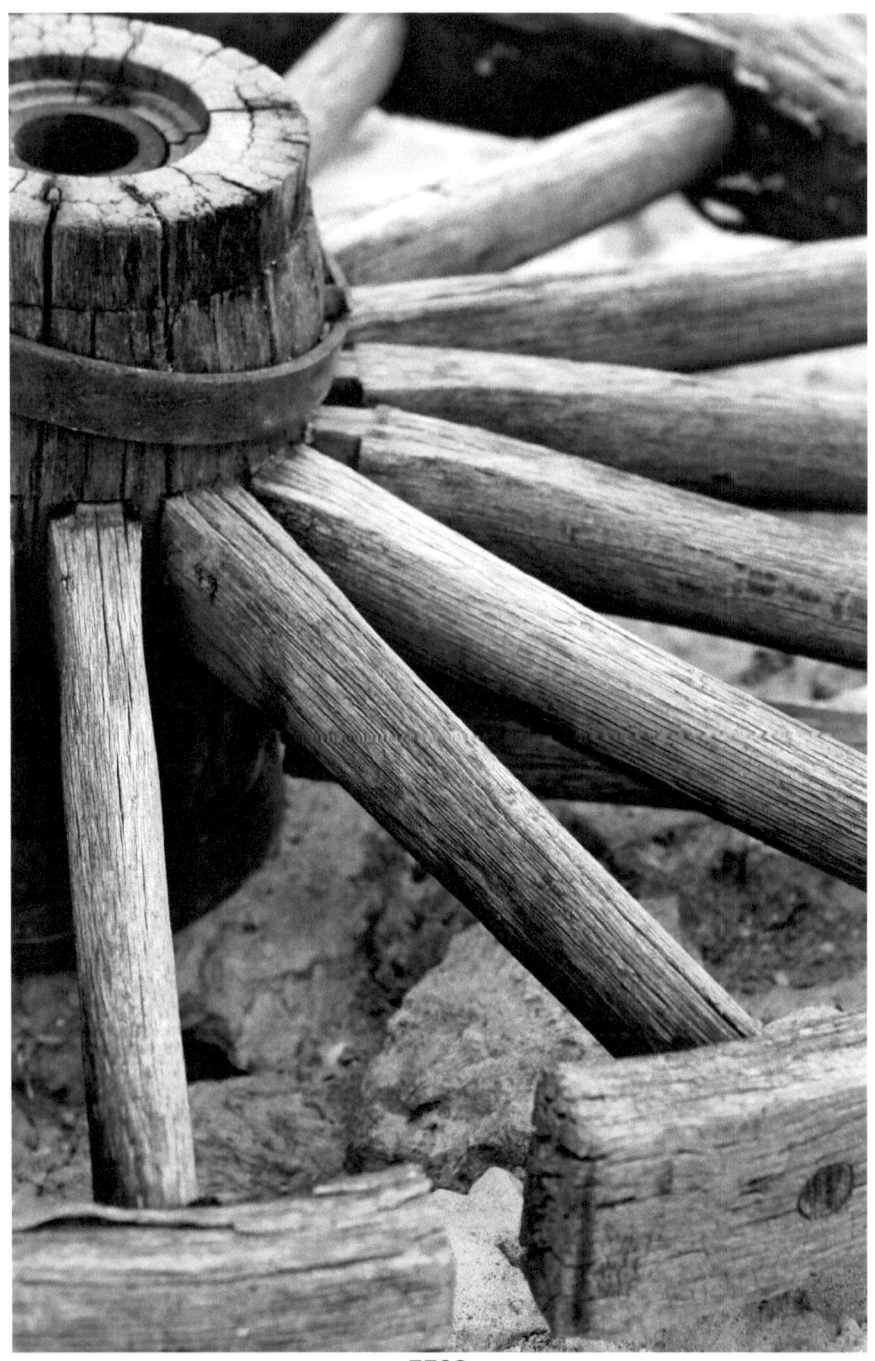

7783

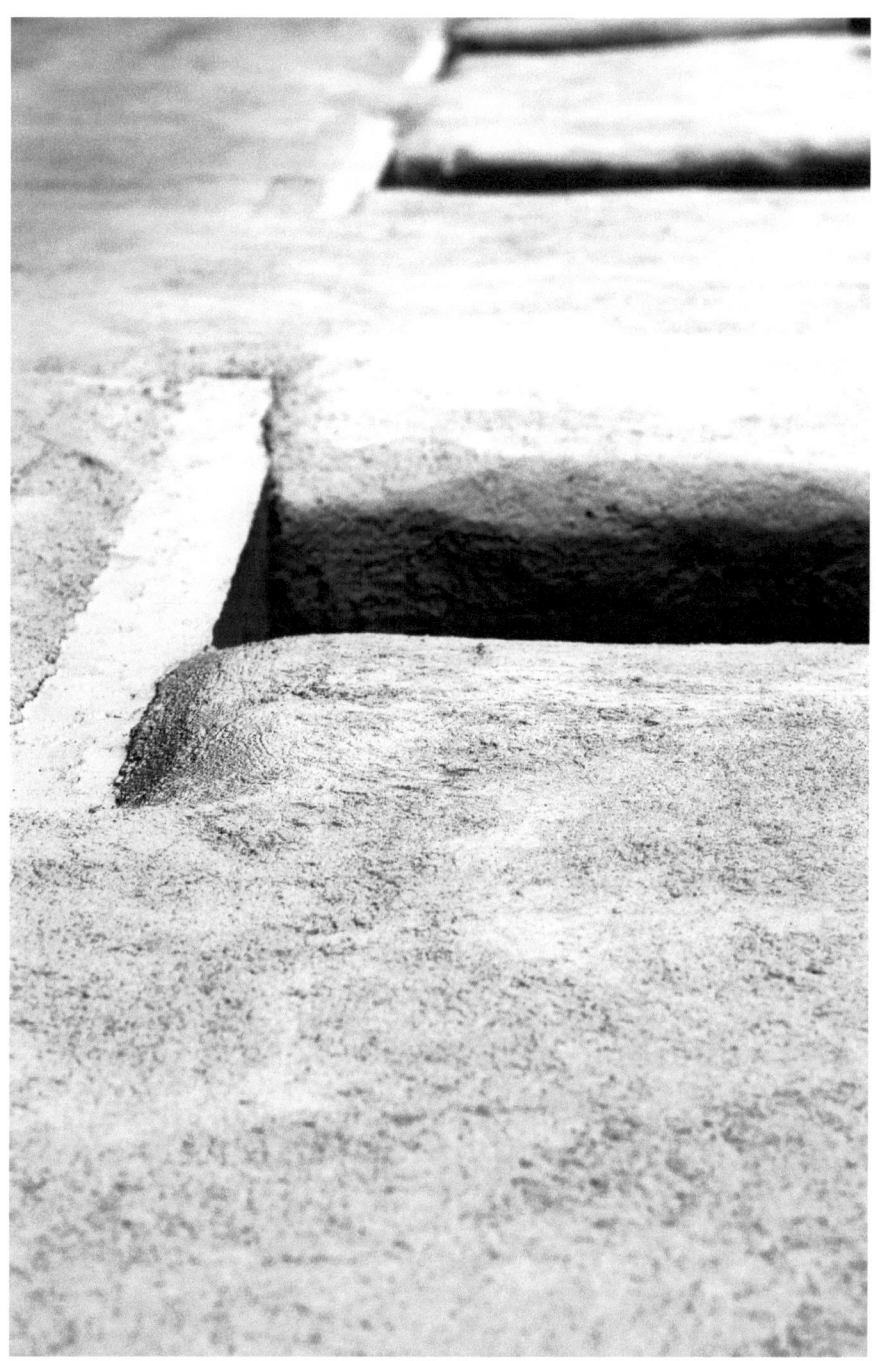

7843

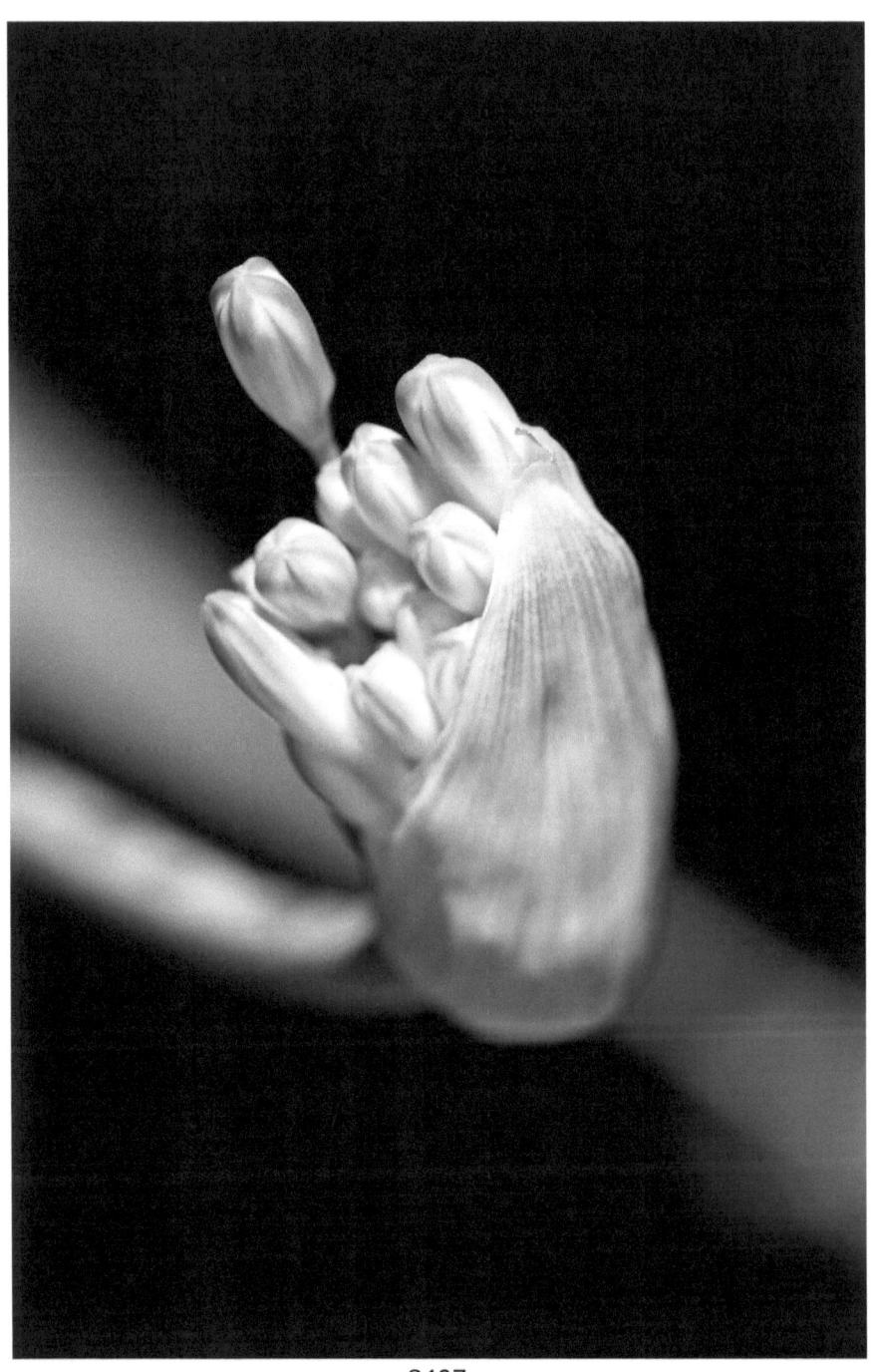

8407

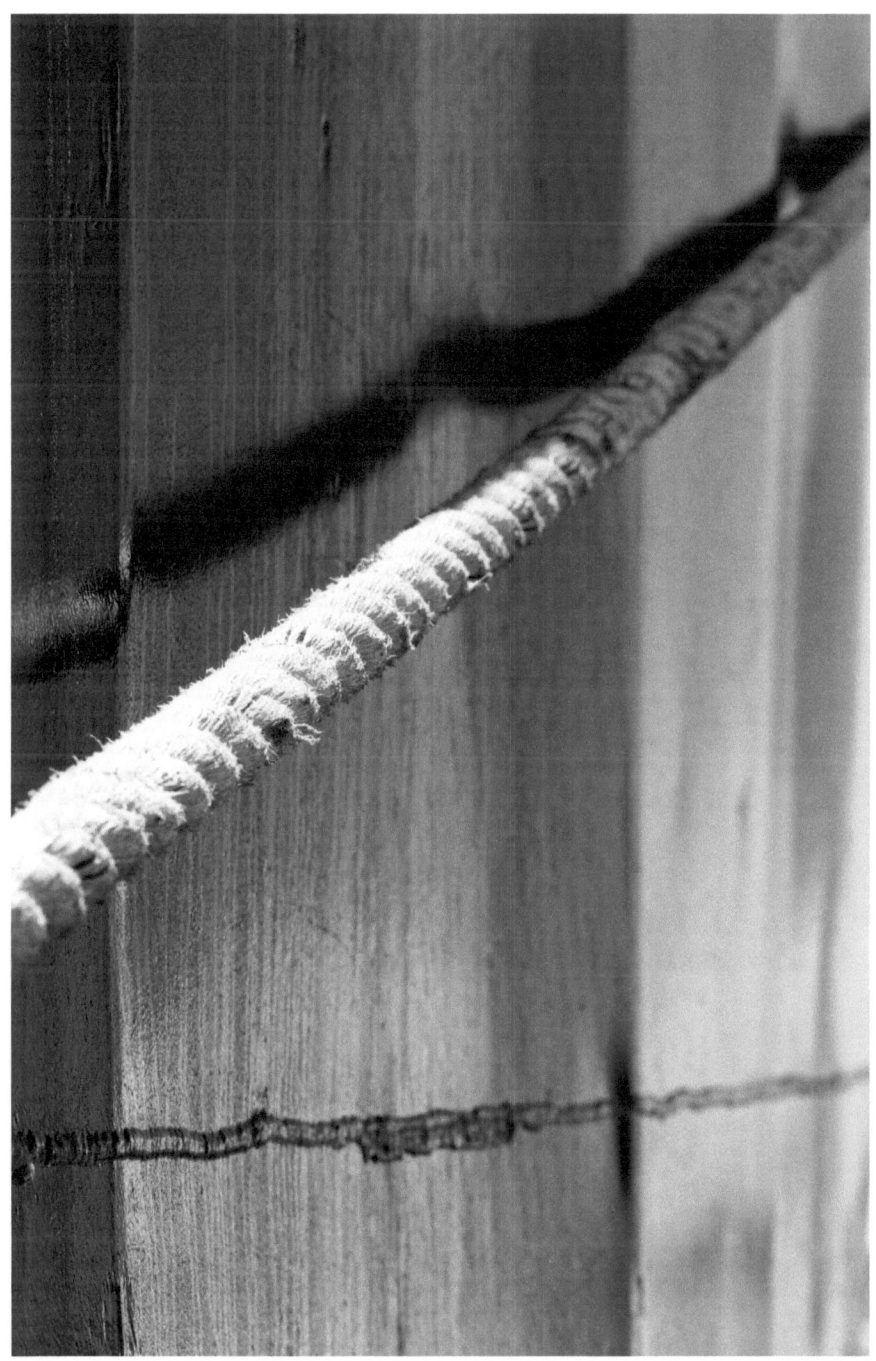

8470

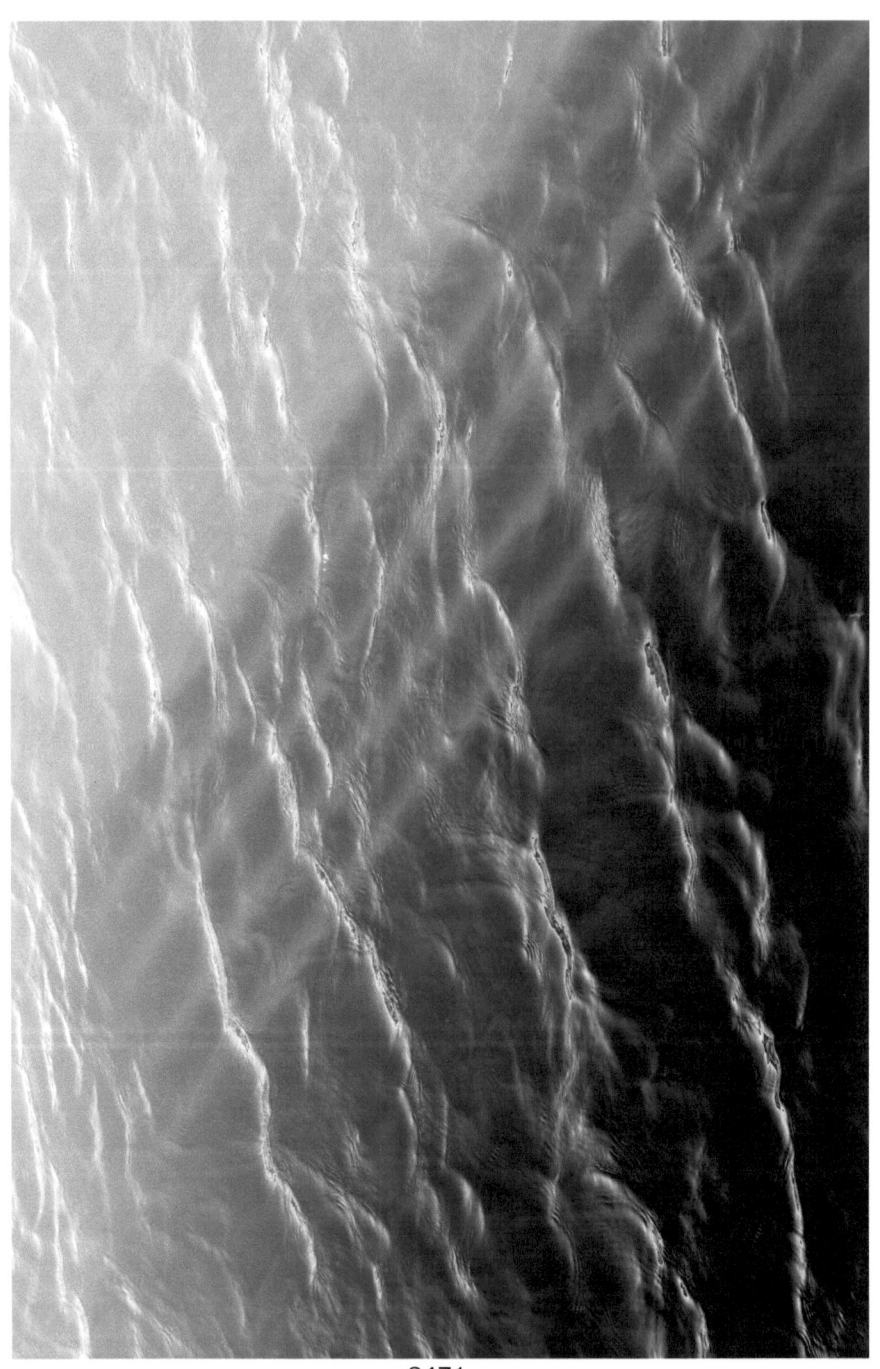

8471

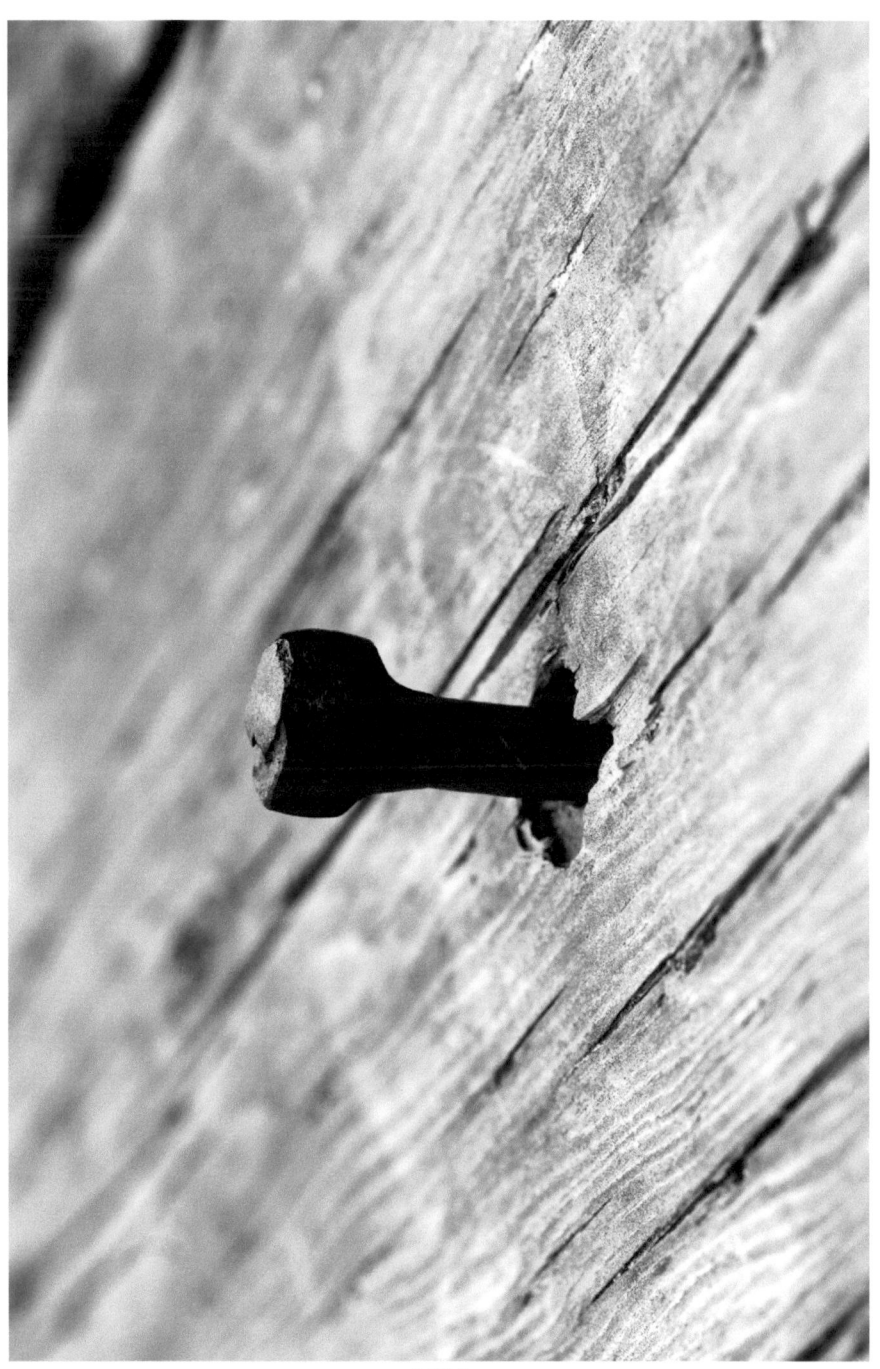

9024

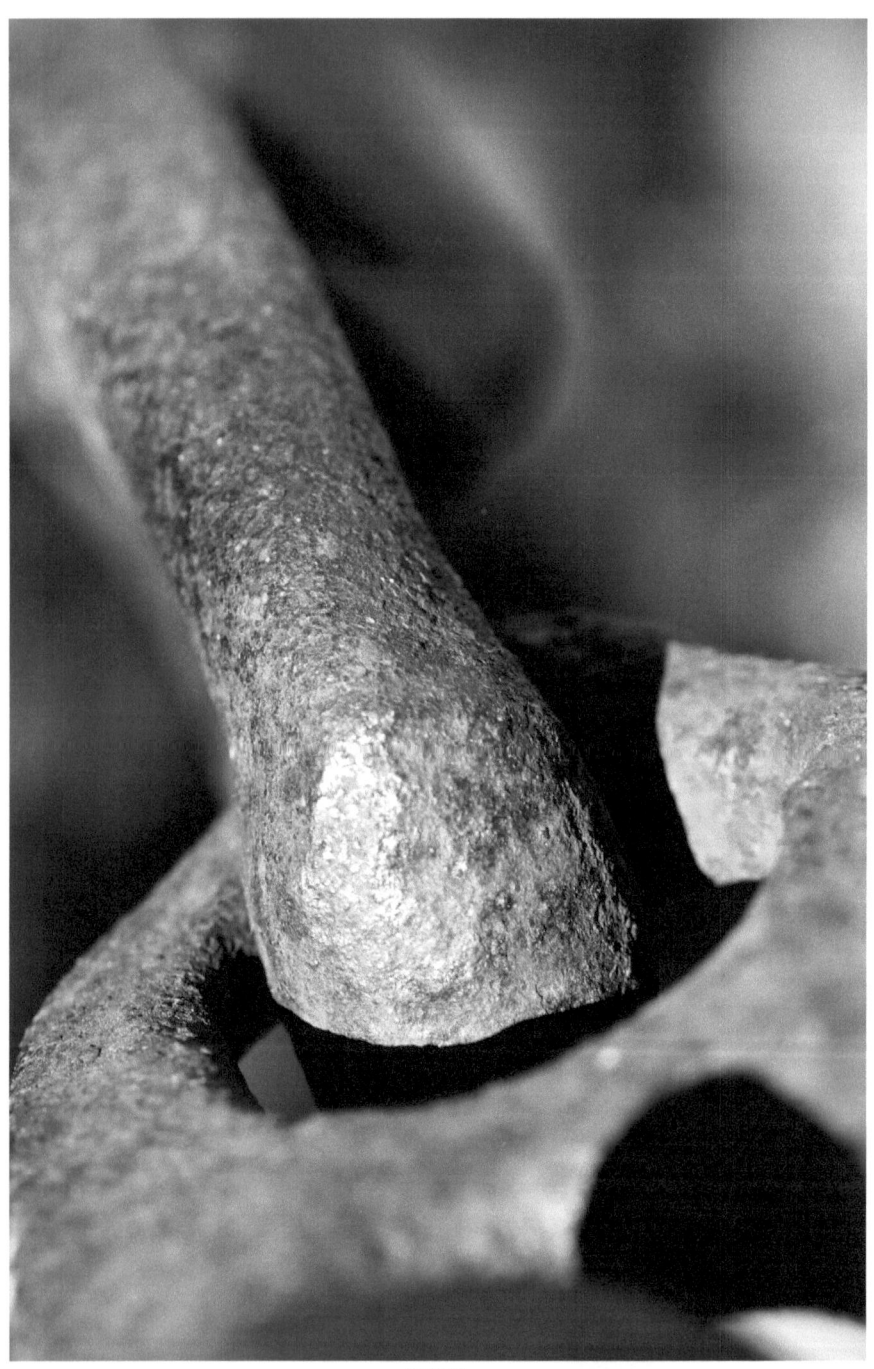

9353

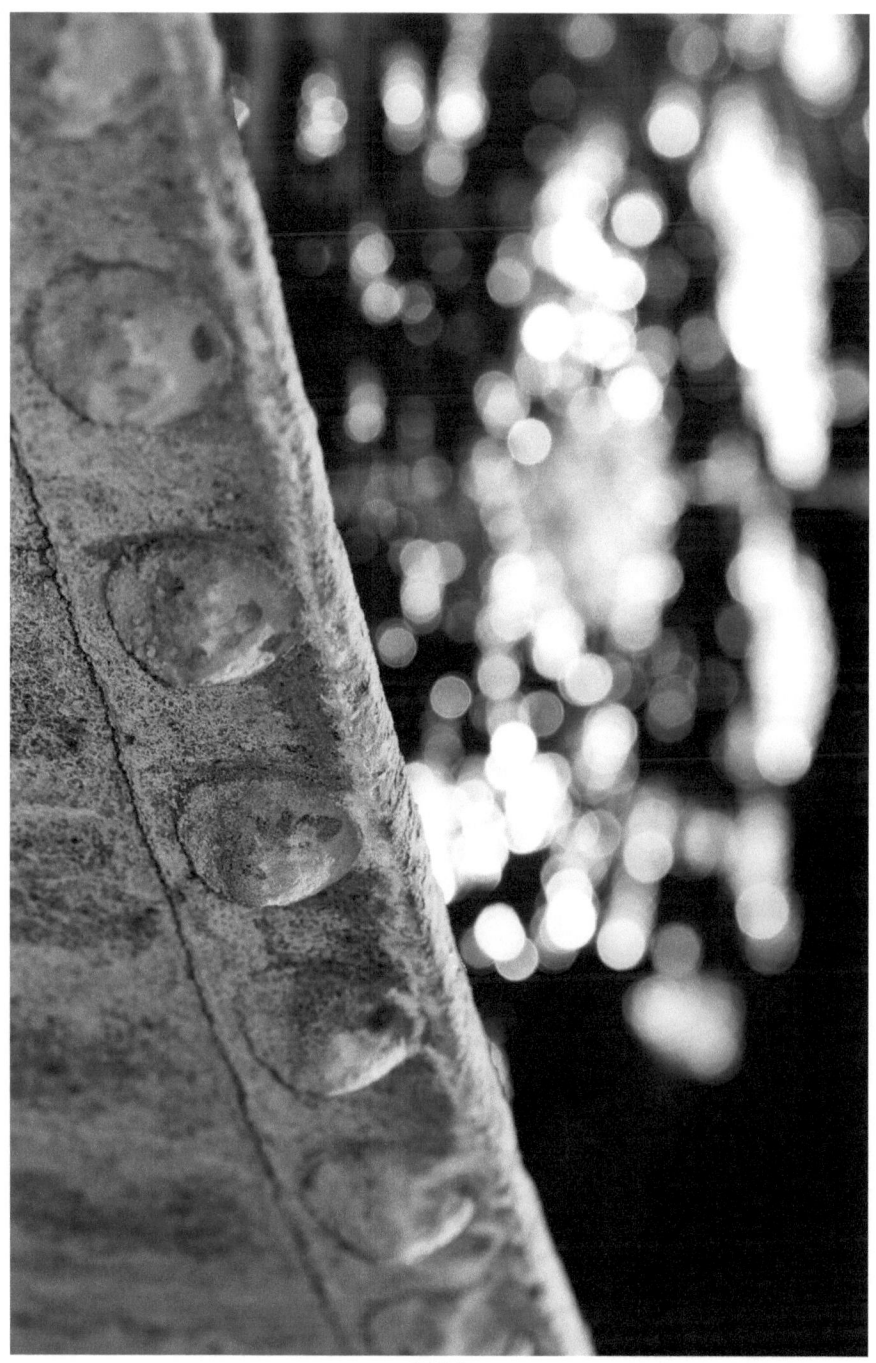

9430

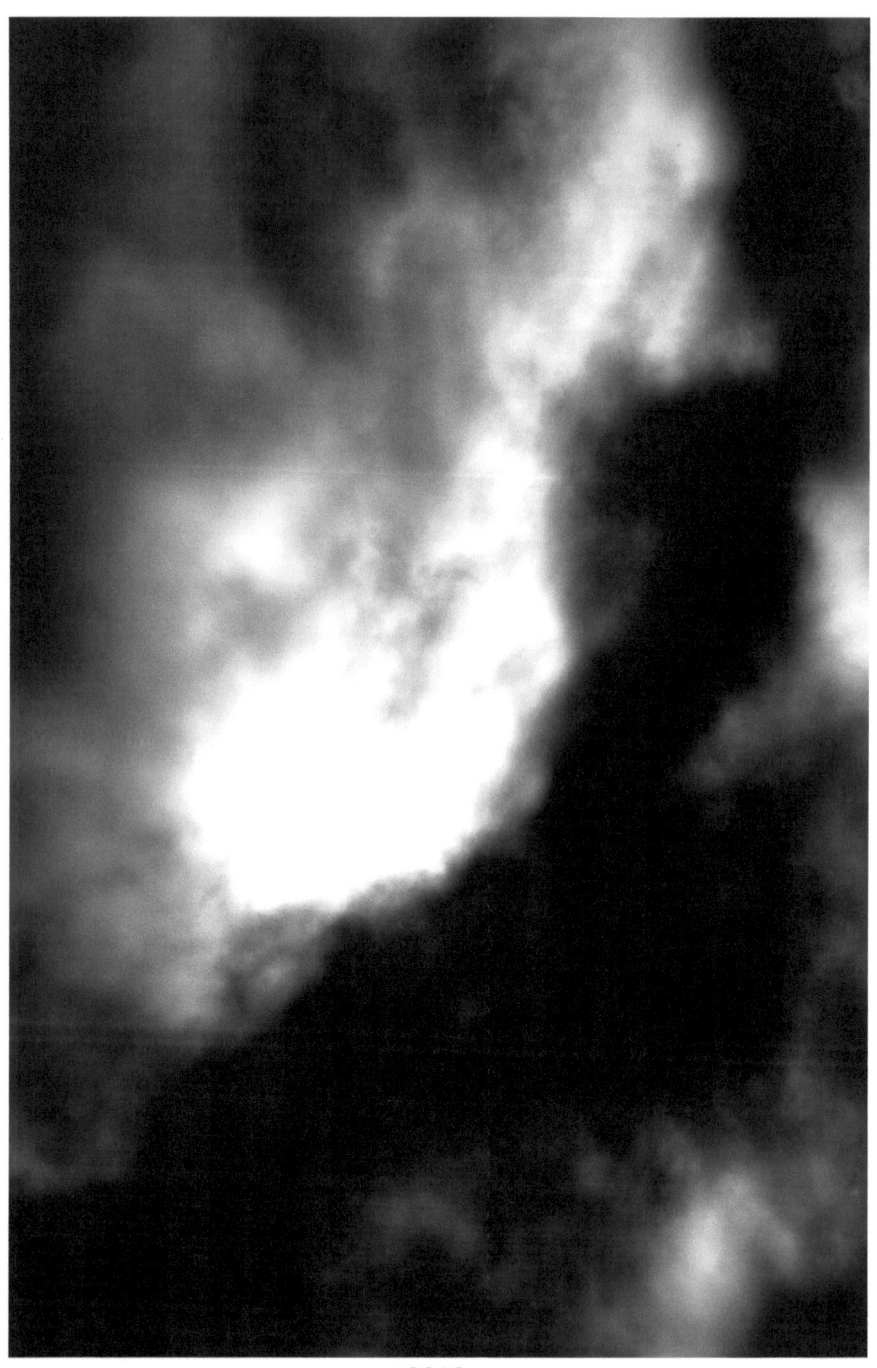

9918

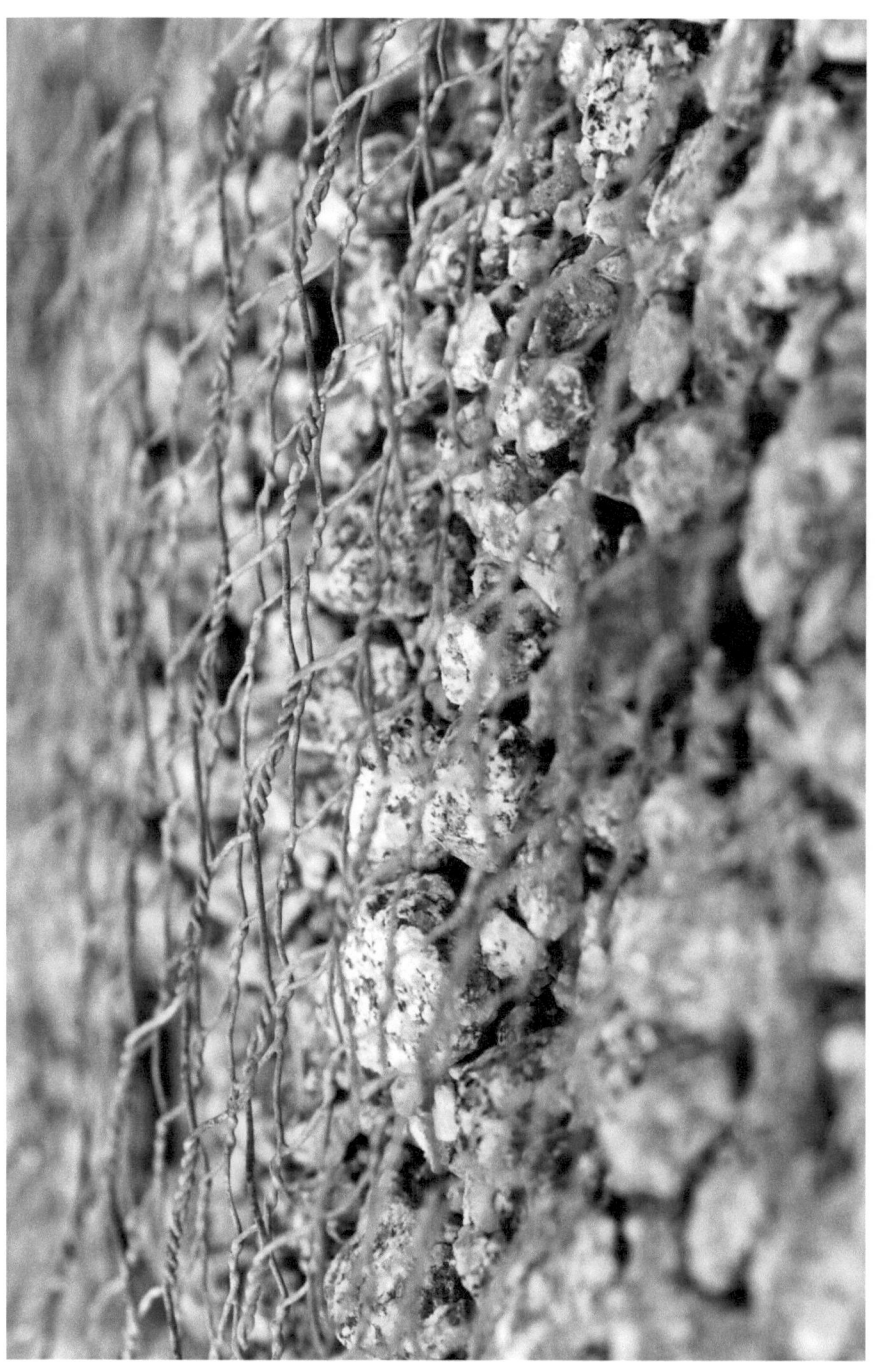

9970

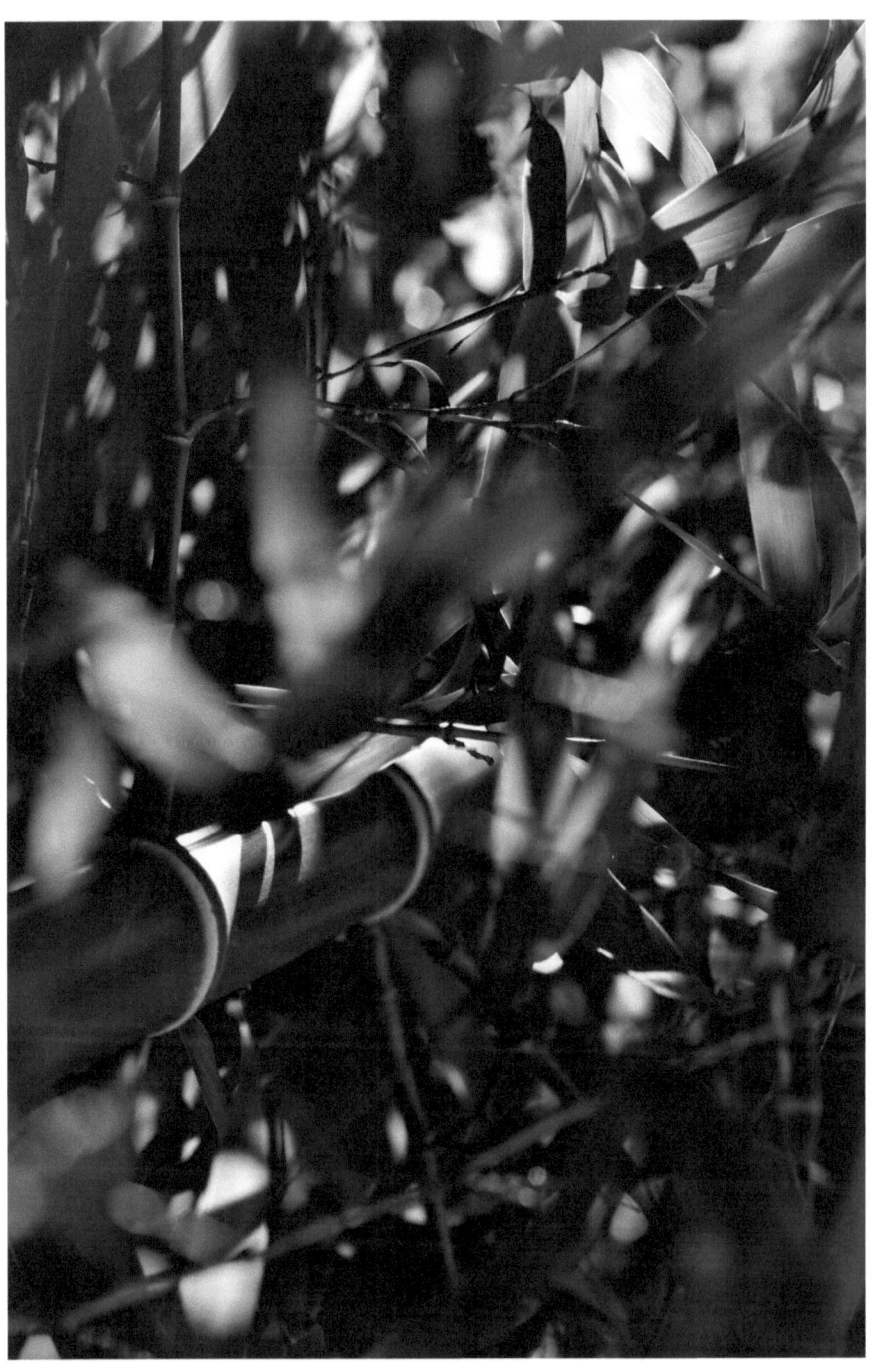

9975

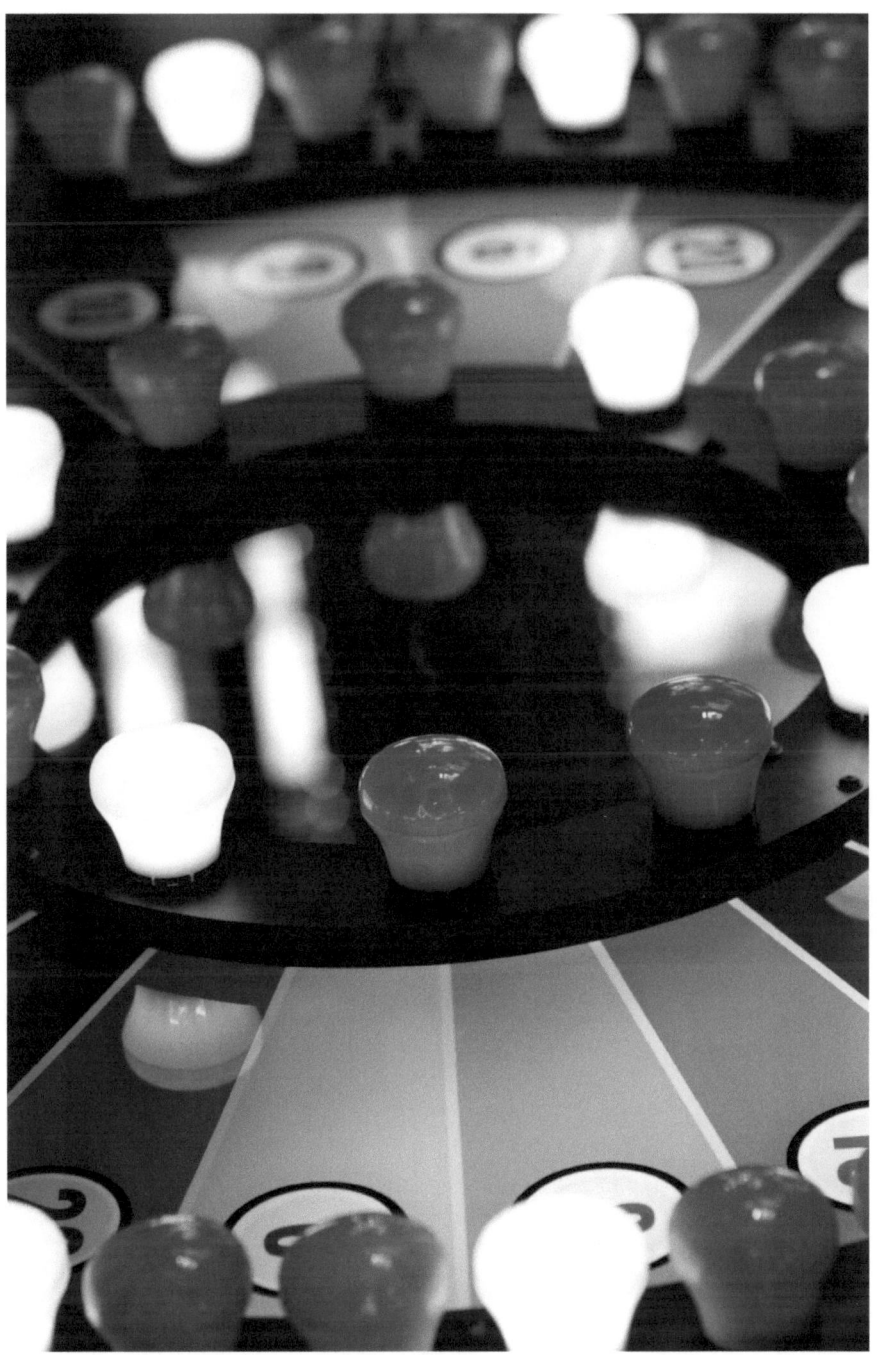

9980

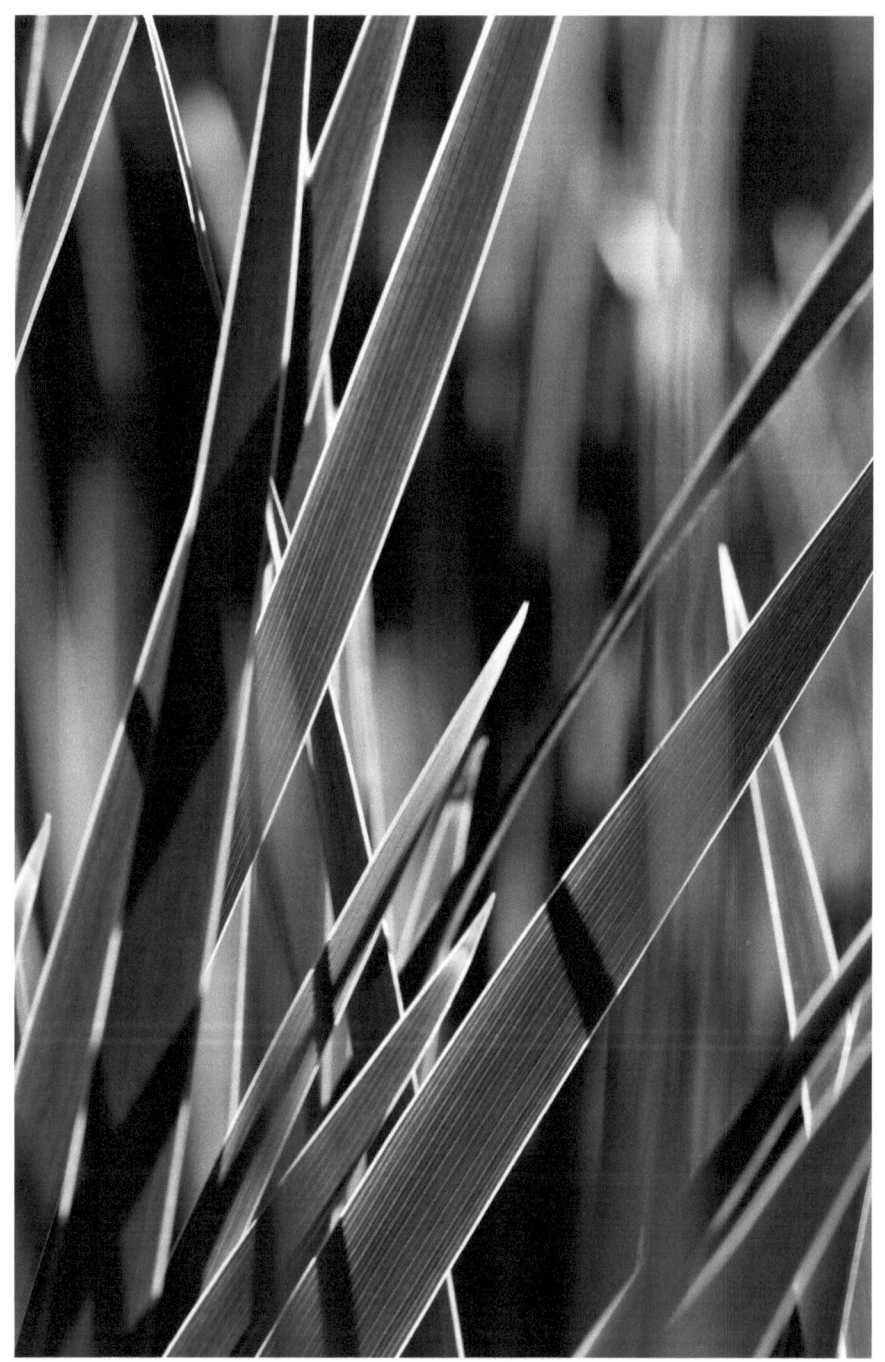

10000

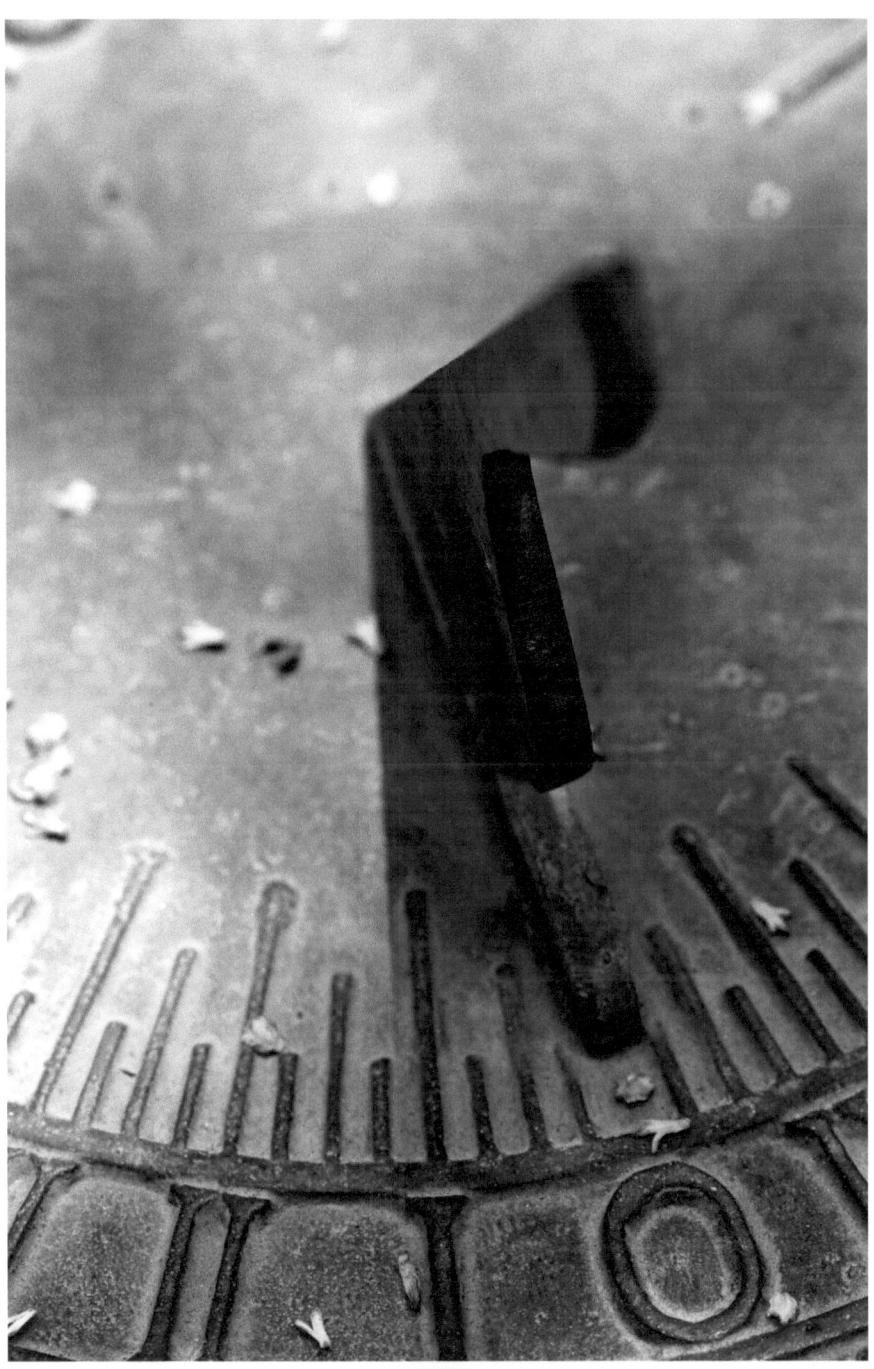

10002

www.ingramcontent.com/pod-product-compliance
Lightning Source LLC
Chambersburg PA
CBHW040921180526
45159CB00002BA/558